C000257671

Scott and Amundsen

Scott
and
Amundsen

Duel in the Ice

RAINER-K. LANGNER

Translated by Timothy Beech

Haus Publishing

Copyright © 2007 Rainer-K. Langner
Translation copyright © 2007 Timothy Beech

First published in Great Britain in 2007 by Haus Publishing,
26 Cadogan Court, Draycott Avenue, London SW3 3BX
www.hauspublishing.co.uk

Originally published as *Duell im ewigen Eis* © Fischer Taschenbuch Verlag,
Frankfurt am Main 2001

Photographs courtesy of Getty Images and Topham Picturepoint

The moral rights of the author have been asserted

A CIP catalogue record for this book is available from the British Library

ISBN 978-1-905791-08-8

Typeset in Garamond 3 by MacGuru Ltd
info@macguru.org.uk
Printed and bound by Graphicom in Vicenza, Italy
Jacket illustration courtesy Getty Images

Contents

The Fram *photographed at the beginning of the voyage that was to take Amundsen and his men to the South Pole. The ship was owned by the Arctic explorer Fridtjof Nansen and loaned to Amundsen for his expedition in 1910.*

1

Arrival of the Gladiators

'I don't hold that anyone but an Englishman should get to the South Pole.'

Robert Falcon Scott

'I don't want to bother you by asking what you think of me as a juggler. My God, if you have to be an acrobat, you must just bite the bullet and become one.'

Roald Amundsen

On 29 November 1910, tugs towed the British ship *Terra Nova* under Captain Robert Falcon Scott out of the harbour of Port Chalmers into the open sea off New Zealand. People threw their hats and caps in the air; on the quay a choir belted out 'God save the King' while the crew on board the expedition ship stood stiffly at attention. It was three o'clock in the afternoon, and the sun shone brightly over the scene. The *Terra Nova* was escorted by small boats crammed with spectators, and by several tugs; the big ship's sailing manoeuvres were rewarded by loud cheering. Then the ship, equipped with both sails and a steam engine, began to make way on its own, leaving behind first the boats, then the tugs. The coast of New Zealand gradually disappeared below the horizon. Not all the men on board would see Port Chalmers again.

They set course towards the mysterious white continent, ever southwards, down the 170th line of longitude east of Greenwich. This imaginary line soon became a zig-zag; the lines of longitude and latitude spread over the Earth by cartographers are just a mathematical abstraction to which the oceans are indifferent. The rigging still cast shadows onto blue-green icebergs, and the crew remained confident – but it was not to be for much longer.

Six weeks previously in Melbourne Scott had caught up with the famous telegram that had already been delivered in Oslo on 3 October; he could not understand its contents: 'I am so bold as to announce that the *Fram* is going to the Antarctic. Amundsen.'

All he knew was that his Norwegian rival had set off with his expedition to explore the Arctic. That was what the newspapers had reported, and the Royal Geographical Society in London had the same information; Amundsen was taking the *Fram* to the North Pole, not the South Pole. An error in transmission? Scott sent a telegram asking Fridtjof Nansen, who ought to know, what Amundsen's goal was. Nansen's answer – 'Unknown' – was both short and disingenuous; he had already known on 1 October the news proclaimed the following day in huge letters on the front page of the *Christiania Presse*: 'The *Fram* is sailing full steam ahead to the South Pole! Sensational news from Roald Amundsen! Fridtjof Nansen says: "A wonderful plan! Via the South Pole to the North Pole!"'

Then, at the beginning of November, Scott got the news that the *Fram* was probably making for McMurdo Sound, the same coastal region of the Antarctic continent the *Terra Nova* was heading for. This must have made Scott realise that the British expedition to the South Pole was being challenged to a competition by Amundsen. Did he know what he was letting himself in for? A competition he never wanted to have and that he initially concealed from his men. But where was Amundsen now? Also according to London, the *Fram* had left Madeira under full sail in the second week of September. It was difficult to know what to make of this; more than two months had passed since then. So where was Amundsen now? It was clear to Scott that if he wanted to beat his competitor to the South Pole, he would have to be the first to anchor in McMurdo Sound. He could not afford to lose his head start.

Two days after Scott sailed from Port Chalmers, the ship ran into a tremendous storm; winds in excess of 100 kilometres per hour drove ten- to twelve-metre high waves over the heavily laden *Terra Nova*. On deck the packing cases containing three motorised sleds broke loose, though they had been carefully tied down. The 19 ponies aboard were flung against the sides of their boxes; the 33 Siberian dogs were put on short chains so they would not be washed overboard by the waves. The ship, hopelessly overburdened, was not prepared to meet such weather. Sacks of coal got soaked and burst. Coal dust mixed with the sea water and the black-brown soup was washed into the hold; rivers of rain flowed down to the keel. Then the pumps broke down, and could not be repaired because it was impossible to open the pump hatch. Now they paid for the fact that this aging system had not been replaced, or at least thoroughly over-hauled, when the *Terra Nova*, a former whaling ship launched in 1884, was being fitted out for the expedition. Scott had cut the wrong corner; he had a refrigeration chamber installed in the ship, for a considerable sum, in order to transport enough meat to the Antarctic cold for the crew of 72 and for the dogs: 162 slaughtered sheep, three cows, tinned milk, veal kidneys, carefully stored in three tons of ice. A few extra boxes of ammunition would have been a cheaper means of providing fresh meat on the spot – from seals and penguins. But this meant there was no money left to pay for effective pumps. Scott may also not have been expecting to encounter such conditions, or he may have believed British seamanship could cope with all weathers.

As the water level rose inexorably, it put out the boiler fire, and by the early hours of the morning the *Terra Nova*, 57 metres long and 9.5 metres wide, was being tossed about on the raging sea with no means of steering. Setting sail was out of the question; the rigging had been torn from the masts. The crew, huddled together in a tiny space below decks, awaited orders from the leader of the expedition, but Scott had none to give, at least no practicable ones. The water

Scott's ship the Terra Nova *anchored in the Antarctic 1911.*

rose, wave after wave crashed over the ship, pushing the gunwales under the water – with ever-increasing frequency. The frightened ponies emptied their bladders and their guts, so that urine and faeces seeped through the decks and fell onto the sailors. Nobody cared. Some clasped their hands in prayer.

It was Scott's second-in-command, Teddy Evans, who had a hole cut in a bulkhead to reach the intake of the defective pump. Seamen, many of whom tore off their clothes, stood up to their necks in water for ten hours to form a bucket chain to get the dirty soup out of the engine room. The crew were shaken out of their lethargy, even though more water was streaming into the hold than they could manage to get out. Then Teddy Evans got the pumps going again, but that brought no immediate improvement.

The storm raged for 36 hours, and then, finally, silence reigned. The *Terra Nova* would not have been able to keep afloat any longer. While the crew were applauding Teddy Evans, Captain Scott noted the results of the inferno in the logbook. 'Two ponies lost, one dog, 65 gallons of oil, ten tons of coal, one of the biologist's jars of alcohol, a large piece of railing from the aft deck, and about ten feet of forward bulkhead wall.' The *Terra Nova* had survived. Then he thanked Evans sincerely, praising his efforts in front of the crew. Scott kept it to himself that he would have preferred to be the one to receive their praise.

Life on board returned to normal. Officers and scientists took their meals in the tiny officers' mess; the crew scrubbed the decks in strict accordance with British naval regulations.

65 degrees 8 minutes South, 177 degrees 41 minutes West. The first icebergs and pack ice. On 9 December the *Terra Nova* ran into the pack ice that encircles the Antarctic like a fortification. This desert, consisting of lumps of ice about one metre across and mighty table icebergs, was familiar to Scott from 1902, the year when he was on the way to the Antarctic continent on board the *Discovery*. Then he had got through the barrier without any difficulty; in September, the winter month of the southern half of the globe, the ice covered about 20 million square kilometres of the ocean surface, melting down to about four million square kilometres by February, the Antarctic midsummer. But on this occasion, things were different. The crew barely noticed a flock of penguins that jumped out of the narrow strips of water between the lumps of ice on to its surface. The *Terra Nova* was crashing heavily against the ice, forcing its hull to search out a navigable channel between the individual sharp-edged fragments. Ice floes got under the bows, and if they did not break under the weight of the ship, the engine had to be stopped while the crew carefully manoeuvred backwards. Frequently individual bergs pushed up against the side of the ship, and had to be laboriously fended off with boat hooks. The whole frame of the ship juddered and groaned, moaning and bending under the pressure of the white wasteland. The ice field into which the *Terra Nova* was pushing itself would snap with a sharp report like a gunshot, when it broke

under the weight of the ship. The pack ice moved with the currents of the sea, unpredictably. Scott thought he was in a game of chance that, as he often feared, might cost the ship its propeller. 'The worst conditions a ship ever had.' Table icebergs, some of them 25 metres high, passed dangerously close. Again and again the boiler was put out to save coal. Yet the situation was changing from one moment to the next. The lookout in the crow's nest at the top of the mast might report open water, and the fire would be lit and the engine revved up; meanwhile, the ice would have closed in once more. 'It is quite inexplicable that we are encountering pack ice so much further north than we expected.' Morale on board, however, was better than the captain recorded it as being. A few penguins were shot.

On Christmas Day, the boat was decorated with flags, and hymns could be heard over the white wastes. Christmas dinner was served in the officers' mess: tomato soup, steamed penguin breast, asparagus, roast beef, plum pudding, mince pies, champagne, port and liqueurs. 'We were at table for five hours singing cheery songs. The crew had their dinner around twelve with more or less the same food, but with beer and a bit of whisky.' This further improved morale. God save the King and the *Terra Nova*, still not out of the ice. The whole ship became covered in a thin layer of ice, over every plank and every rope.

It was only after three weeks, at 72 degrees 17 minutes South, 177 degrees 9 minutes West, that the pack ice released the *Terra Nova*. 'All in all it took us twenty days and a few hours to get through the pack ice; as the crow flies, we have covered 680 kilometres, 34 kilometres a day. Out of 20 days we were under steam for nine. Shackleton would certainly never have reached this southern sea if he had got into the pack ice like that.' There, once again, was the rivalry from the days when the two were sailing on the *Discovery* together. Then, in 1902, Scott, Ernest Shackleton and the zoologist Dr Edward Wilson, chief of the expedition's scientific staff, were on the way to the South Pole. They managed to reach 82 degrees 17 minutes South, 300 kilometres further than any of them had got before. Then that was it and Scott had sent Shackleton back to England against his wishes. Shackleton was resentful, and that made Scott resentful in turn. In January 1909 Shackleton had got to within 175 kilometres of the Pole with an expedition of his own, and now Scott wanted to conquer the last little bit. It would all be over and Scott would have won. Perhaps that was why he had completely forgotten about the third man, Roald Amundsen, because he was competing in a purely British field.

Towards noon, the *Terra Nova* was sailing further south-wards in the open Ross Sea as the ice dropped from the rigging, crashing on to the deck and melting in the sunlight. Some of the men drew buckets of seawater over the gunwales to have a bath with salt water soap while others sat around. In the evening, the crew sighted the Antarctic continent at a distance of around 210 kilometres, the shining peak of Mount Erebus, at the entrance to the McMurdo Sound. This was where the ship would anchor. 'Considering the unusual conditions we ran into, it may well be said that things could have been far worse.' He had no way of knowing that Amundsen was already hard on his heels.

On 9 September 1910, when the *Terra Nova* had already left Cape Town, 5,000 nautical miles from Madeira, the *Fram* raised anchor without a great deal of fuss at nine o'clock in the evening – earlier than usual. Amundsen always set off on his expeditions at a late hour. By dawn he wanted to have reached the only place where he felt he came to life, miles away from humdrum routine: on the high seas, bound by no horizon. Later it would be said that Roald Amundsen and the other 18 men of the *Fram*'s crew sneaked out of Funchal, Madeira's port. In the wheelhouse of that gem of Norwegian shipbuilding hung a map of the Antarctic, with the destination of the voyage marked on it: the Bay of Whales in the Ross Sea ice barrier, about 150 kilometres nearer to the South Pole, as Amundsen had explained to his men, than any other place that could be reached by ship, a whole degree further south than Scott could hope for, since his destination was going to be in McMurdo Sound. This was a stroke of strategic genius in the part of the Norwegian, who had made a careful study of the results of all previous expeditions to the subpolar continent.

The first circumnavigation of the Antarctic had been completed by James Clark Ross in the *Erebus* and the *Terror* some 70 years before. Firmly believing that the Antarctic region was made up of small ice-covered islands, so that the Pole could be reached by sea, he repeatedly made for the pack ice, looking for a way through. On 9 January 1841 he sighted the end points of a mighty chain of mountains that he named 'Victoria Land', after his queen. As far as the pack ice permitted, Ross sailed southwards right under the coast of the Transantarctic Mountains through an ice-free sea that would be named the 'Ross Sea' after its discoverer. His hope grew with each mile that the two ships covered, until it was shattered by a precipitous, unconquerable barrier of ice. There it lay, at the foot of a volcano, Mount Erebus, drawing endlessly away from the mountain formation eastwards – ice, pushed down into the ocean bay from the Antarctic mountains, with a sharp edge, sticking straight up 20 metres, twice as high in places. In all, 540,000 square metres of ice shelf sealed the continent off from the Ross Sea, a white, icy waste, one and a half times the size of Germany. Ross still did not give up; he vainly hoped to find the vital gap in this wall of ice by sailing to the east. Huge masses of ice would often break off its high flank and crash into the sea, so the sailors had to be on their guard. The spray rose up above the height of the mast; individual fragments hailed down on the crew like shrapnel, and when fog turned the mighty object into something out of hell, Ross ordered a new course to be set – north.

For more than six decades no sailor desired to follow Sir James Clark Ross into this hell. In 1895, the British whaler *Antarctic* entered the Ross Sea, and from the crow's nest the Norwegian Carsten Borchgrevink, a boyhood friend of Roald Amundsen, saw a strip of ice-free land on Cape Adare, the northern point of Victoria Land, sticking out into the sea. On 23 January 1895, Borchgrevink was the first man to walk on dry land in Antarctica. Four years later he returned to Cape Adare as the leader of a privately-financed British-Norwegian expedition; he and his men were the first to winter in the Antarctic. He sailed along the great ice barrier on the *Southern Cross*, more than 700 kilometres eastwards, up to the place that Ross had identified as an inlet in the shelf ice. The *Southern Cross* anchored here, and Borchgrevink set off on the first march towards the South Pole. On 17 February 1900, he reached 78 degrees 50 minutes South before having to turn back.

In 1902 Scott happened upon the same place while looking for a landing place on the *Discovery*, but he thought the inlet was not suitable for a base camp. Because of the dubious ice conditions he picked the western end of the Ross Barrier, the McMurdo Sound, as his expedition headquarters, where the edge of the ice shelf descends to sea level.

In 1908, when Shackleton sought to anchor at the spot from which Borchgrevink had marched some 100 kilometres to the south, the inlet that he had seen himself on the *Discovery* six years previously had disappeared. A piece of the ice shelf several miles across had broken off and been driven out to sea. In this ice wall was a great crack just wide enough to pass through. Behind it the opening must get wider, as Shackleton could make out the humps of many whales. But no-one would be foolish enough to manoeuvre his ship into this Bay of Whales. Shackleton wrote in his diary: 'The thought of what might have been made me decide then and there that under no circumstances would I winter on the Barrier and that wherever we did land we would secure a solid rock foundation for our winter home.' So Shackleton returned to where he had already been with Scott, McMurdo Sound, on the coast of Victoria Land.

Amundsen, who was familiar with Scott's plans for the South Pole, which had been published in *The Times* in 1909, thought the British scheme of conquering the Pole from the McMurdo Sound just an unimaginative repetition of what had been tried before. He felt that setting up his headquarters where others had fought shy of the danger of being driven out to sea was terribly adventurous. After all, his childhood companion Borchgrevink had taken the first steps towards the South Pole from that very spot. 'I had carefully studied this formation on the Ice Barrier, and come to the conclusion that what is known as the Bay of Whales is the very same inlet that James Clark Ross observed, although major changes have occurred. This formation had been in the same place for 70 years. So I said to myself that it could be no accident – it was no whim of nature that had brought this enormous stream of ice to a stop at this precise spot, but *terra firma*, allowing a permanent inlet to form in the ice front which normally moves slowly along.'

Although the Bay of Whales does not in fact lie over dry land, and though the ice surrounding it moves along like the ice shelf throughout the Ross Sea, Amundsen had drawn the right conclusion from the available reports. On a human timescale, the Bay of Whales is indeed a permanent formation in the ice shelf. Departing for the Pole from there would give an advantage of about 150 kilometres over setting off from the McMurdo Sound, and Amundsen did not want to lose this advantage; however, there was still some risk. The movements of the ice shelf had not yet been scientifically analysed, and its formation had only been described in the eyewitness reports of a few travellers. Amundsen could not be totally certain, but he knew from experience that the situation in the ice could change from one moment to the next; nonetheless, he chose the Bay of Whales as the starting point for his attempt on the Pole. If the ice broke and his base camp drifted out on to the Ross Sea, he and his men would be lost. Amundsen knew this and still picked this relatively risky place. It was victory that counted, not survival.

In the knowledge that they would already have the advantage over their competitor once they had reached the shelf ice, 19 men crossed the equator with their dogs, with pigs, hens, cats, sheep and Fridtjof the canary, who had been taken along as a mascot. Morale aboard the *Fram* was as it should be, and this suited Amundsen. Scott paid strict attention to the rank of his people and to the maintenance of naval discipline; the *Terra Nova* was a navy ship. But daily life on the *Fram* was organized on a more companionable basis. Jobs that needed to be done were shared equally according to a rota, by everyone including Amundsen himself. But it was the boss alone, Roald Amundsen, who decided what needed to be done and when; all 18 men had placed themselves absolutely under his authority, with a handshake and also by signing a written contract. There was no room for criticism of his leadership, and Amundsen was cold and unforgiving when he heard of it, as one of the crew would later discover – he was eventually to shoot himself.

The food on the *Fram* was good and abundant; they were constantly winding up the record player or browsing in the library, which contained nearly three thousand books, and they made use of the time to make improvements to the equipment. 'If we want to win, not a single button must be out of place', the boss said. When the ship passed 40 degrees South, the Greenland dogs were taken off their chains after they had been muzzled to prevent them from tearing one another to pieces. 'Before untying the dogs, we had noticed that some were not as happy as they should have been. They were anxious and more nervous than the others. When they were free we saw what was the matter with them. They had old friends that happened to have been kept in a different corner, and the reason for their grief was this separation. It was moving to watch their joy at being reunited with their friends. The animals had changed completely. Naturally, we made sure that they were in the same teams in future' After a few days the muzzles were taken off the dogs and they were allowed to roam freely. After two months more at sea, 21 dogs were born. Female puppies were killed, but the males were kept; within a year they would have grown into powerful sled dogs. Everything was subordinated to the great aim of reaching the South Pole before Scott, even the dogs' lives.

The *Fram* struggled on, crashing and weaving its way southwards; she had not been built for journeys such as this, with her round, bulging hull. For almost three years, from 1893 to 1896, the ship had lain trapped in the Arctic pack ice drifting as though imprisoned from the New Siberian Islands to Spitzbergen. That was what Fridtjof Nansen had built her for, double-hulled and round, to prevent the ice from getting a grip on his ship. Nansen's drift expedition, an adventure that no-one would have risked before, made him and the *Fram* world famous. Now Amundsen was captain of the *Fram*, and he steered her half way round the globe without putting in at another port – 14,000 nautical miles. On 3 January 1911, just short of four months after they had left Funchal, the ship entered the Antarctic pack ice at 175 degrees 35 minutes East. The *Fram*, like its crew, was in her element, and now only 300 miles behind the *Terra Nova*. The new diesel motor ensured swift progress, being capable of delivering full power immediately if needed, unlike *Terra Nova*'s engine which had to raise steam before the propeller could be engaged. The men shot seals so that the dogs could eat their fill of meat and blubber before being harnessed to the sledges. It only took the *Fram* three days to get through the pack ice, and all eyes looked to the south. On 11 January the crewman Olav Bjaaland, the Norwegian cross-country and ski-jumping champion, wrote in his diary: 'Today at last the Ice Barrier is in sight. It gives you a funny feeling to see it lying there. The sea is as calm as a duckpond, and there it is, this Great Wall of China gleaming in the sunlight. Far off, it's like a freshly developed photo.' Amundsen's reaction was more prosaic: There it was – this damned 200 foot high wall of snow – it cannot be called an ice wall – sparkling away at us. I had thought it would make more of an impression on me, but the excellent reproductions in Shackleton's book must have already made it familiar to me, and I regarded it as an old acquaintance. So here we are.'

Three days later, on 14 January, Amundsen steered his ship past sheer ice cliffs into the Bay of Whales, which no-one had previously dared to do. Sometimes, the ice scraped against the hull. Ahead, whales could be seen blowing spouts of water into the air while seals stretched out on the ice, and penguins thronged around as if to greet the newcomers. They had finally got there. The *Fram* was moored with ice anchors on the narrow strip of ice, and after their long journey men and dogs acclimatized their sea legs to the shining white land, *terra incognita*.

'The ice went up to the Ice Barrier via a narrow, level slope, an ideal connection. We continued towards the southeast, and after approximately 15 minutes we reached one of the edge formations on the barrier. These formations resembled terminal moraines with some irregularities at the top. I chose a place in a small valley, fine, level ground, about four nautical miles from the sea. This is where we will erect our hut, and this will be the base for our tasks. Tomorrow, Sunday, we will start to get ready, so that we can get straight to work on Monday.'

When Amundsen set off from Christiania (modern Oslo)

on 3 June 1910, he had estimated the distance from this bay to be 16,000 nautical miles, and set an arrival date of 15 January 1911; after one of the longest sea voyages in the history of polar exploration the *Fram* had arrived one day early, having covered 15,938 nautical miles.

The first battle had been won, and he would now prepare himself for those to come. His trump card was decisive: he knew where his rival would begin his march to the Pole, but Scott could only guess where Amundsen had landed; he did not know for certain. The Norwegians were hidden away in the Bay of Whales. 'There are plenty of seals here, many more then we need for men and animals together. Everything seems to have been arranged to suit us. May God, whom I have learned to love, keep it that way!' Faith alone is not enough to get a ship across the oceans, or to bring it an inch nearer to the Pole. Whatever happened would happen because of him, the heir of a clan that had always kept a tight hold on its own fate.

Captain Scott on skis as the expedition to the South Pole from Cape Evans began. The polar clothing manufactured for the explorers would prove to be hopelessly inadequate.

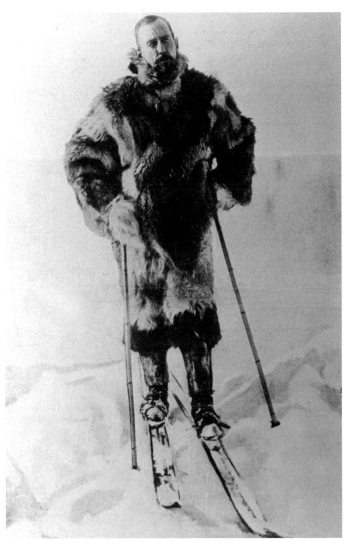

Roald Amundsen photographed in the fur suit that offered far greater warmth and protection against the relentless polar climate.

2

Paths to the Cold

'Norwegian seamen are a solid lot,
Full of strength and cunning more than most;
Wherever ship can swim, they lead the way.'

Bjørnstjerne Bjørnson

'Far-called, our navies melt away;
On dune and headland sinks the fire:
Lo, all our pomp of yesterday,
Is one with Nineveh and Tyre!'

Rudyard Kipling

In 1854 two men from Hvidsten, a dot on a subsidiary channel of the Christiania Fjord, bought a burntout whaler as scrap. One had a shipyard, the other a captain's certificate. When they had fixed up the sailing ship, they named her the *Phoenix*, showing their feeling for the symbolic. Under the command of the 43-year-old captain, her maiden voyage was to the Black Sea. At this time the guns were firing on the Crimean Peninsula, and cavalry divisions clashed on horseback. The Russian Tsar Nicholas I was at war with Turkey, on whose side France and Britain had intervened. The *Phoenix* was moored in Sebastopol and served as winter quarters for British officers; later she was used to transport fodder and straw into the war zone on behalf of the Allies. In 1856, once the war had been decided in favour of the Allies, the ship sailed back to Hvidsten, loaded to the gunwales with the war profits of a 'non-combatant' shared by both men. In this way Jens Engebreth Amundsen, captain and joint owner of the *Phoenix*, laid the foundations of his considerable fortune, just as all his ancestors had done.

Jens Amundsen's ancestors, who had been sailors and shipowners for three or four generations, came from Hvaler, a small group of islands in the Christiania Fjord; they were respected people, successful and confident without exception, and married well, increasing their property by a substantial dowry each time. Jens Amundsen had founded a shipping company with his three brothers, and 30 merchant ships sailed under its flag, the biggest fleet in the district. Near the port of Sarpsborg, on the Sannesund, they had bought the Hvidsten property together with one of Amundsen's brothers-in-law, and divided it up into lots to build houses for their families. From Hvidsten they set out as proprietors and captains to sell their merchandise. When Jens Amundsen was 43, in 1863, he married the 27-year-old Hanna Henrikke Gustava Sahlqvist, the daughter of an official, who followed her husband to the China Sea in pursuit of the next lucrative deal. Jens Amundsen made a good profit transporting a wide variety of goods from numerous sources between Taiwan and the Chinese mainland; that was what the people of strait-laced Hvidsten said, but they did not know that Amundsen was involved in the slave trade. Even had they known, their opinion of his Far Eastern deals would have been little different. Money is money, and so much the better if it grows.

On one occasion Amundsen's ship, a three-master, had hundreds of Chinese coolies aboard being transported to Havana. On the open sea the human cargo was allowed spells on deck, in groups of twelve at a time. One of the prisoners came at the captain from behind with an axe in his hand. Just as the man was about to strike, the captain turned round, and the blade cut open the right side of his face before sailors could overpower the attacker. Later, when this story was told in the family, no-one ever omitted to mention that Gustava Amundsen had used an ordinary needle and thread to sew up her husband's gaping wound. The captain then addressed the Chinese, giving them the choice of punishing the attacker themselves, or all dying together. The man was hanged by his comrades.

Gustava had provided her husband with a son every two years; the first, Jens Ole Antonius, had been born while they were still in China in 1866. When she was pregnant for the fourth time, she finally returned to Norway where she gave birth to their fourth son on 16 July 1872: Roald Engebreth Gravning Amundsen. Roald, 'the glorious' – a name from Norse mythology. Three months after the birth, the family moved to Villa Uranienborg, 9 Am Uranienborgweg,

Christiania – an excellent address, right behind the royal palace. Gustava Amundsen had also managed to get her husband to enter the trade ministry as a head of department, in keeping with his business success and social status. This change did not make for any significant alteration in his way of life; he continued to go to sea on his own ships, but now this was on behalf of the trade ministry and with its blessing.

Roald Amundsen grew up in Christiania as the son of a respected family that had achieved something, and he was brought up on his father's tales of ships and the sea, debit and credit. Naturally, his father's word was law. That was how things always were with the Amundsens, both on their ships and in their homes. Amundsen senior was certainly energetic, and fully determined only to undertake what could be seen through to the end. 'I prefer you not to get involved in fights,' he had said to his sons, adding: 'But if you must, then hit first and make sure that is enough to end it.' Roald looked up to his father just as Jens, Gustav and Leon did.

In the summer and at Christmas the family went out to Hvidsten, with their father's shipyard on the opposite side of the river. This was an adventure playground where Roald could circumnavigate the globe in his childish imagination. In winter when the Glomma froze over, the brothers skated down the Sannesund or tried out their skis from under the Christmas tree on the slopes. So Roald Amundsen grew up in the care of men who were respected because they were well off, and who had seen something of the world; he grew up on the fjord, at the boundary between water and mountains, between icy winters and short, intense summers.

There were no such contrasts in Scott's childhood; nor had there been any snow. He was not to encounter snow until his first Antarctic expedition – white snow, that is, not the soggy mush that people swore at in the streets of Plymouth. Robert Falcon Scott was born outside the gates of the port city, in Devonport, on 6 June 1868, where Her Majesty's Naval Dockyard as well as the Scott property 'Outlands' were situated. 'Outlands' was a few square yards of land on which a house stood; its charm and pretensions had long since faded, and the family always did find it rather cramped.

'Outlands' and a small Plymouth brewery had been the inheritance left by one Robert Scott from Devonshire, a navy paymaster who had amassed some property from the perks of his job and booty from the Napoleonic Wars, to his four sons. The three eldest entered the Indian Army, with the result that house, land and brewery went to the youngest son, John Edward Scott; he soon sold the brewery, and lived off the proceeds. John Edward grew roses in Devonport, took an interest in agriculture, and was modest in an oddly grumpy way; he assumed the airs of a country gentleman, though his character and origins were not fitted to this role, and his financial resources were insufficient to maintain his lifestyle with any ease.

Mrs Hannah Scott, the sister of a navy captain and the niece of a vice admiral, was her husband's social superior, and she had to feed and clothe all 17 members of the household. She managed it with an equanimity that showed her strength of character, and she did not respond to her husband's outbursts of temper. She was always there for everyone and everything, in a largely gentle way that demonstrated her secret ambition to dominate. Scott, whom his mother called Con, was always vulnerable to gentle, strong women, a rather indecisive man.

Until he was eight Robert Scott was cared for by a governess who was preoccupied by the child's mysterious, probably psychosomatic tendency to fall ill, as his parents were too. He often felt sick, and his entire constitution seemed to be worryingly weak. Everyone wanted him to grow up to be a physically robust man, but it was not at all clear that he would. After his governess, Con was sent to the day school in Plymouth, where he was often teased by his schoolmates as the delicate son of a rose breeder. It must have been the smiling patience he inherited from his mother that helped Scott to bear the bullying of his peers, until his father withdrew him from the school and sent him to boarding school. John Scott did not take this decision because he wanted to support his eldest son, but because he was unhappy with his schoolwork.

It was the family tradition that the firstborn should enter the navy, while the other sons entered the army and prepared themselves for a life in some far-flung corner of the Empire. It was as if Scott's father wanted him to make up for the naval career he had been denied because he had to take over the brewery; Captain Robert Falcon Scott, instead of Captain John Edward Scott. But his progress at the Plymouth town school was not good enough for that, so he sent his son to boarding school; he would rather have been giving orders at sea than accepting his wife's gentle demands at home. Con was not asked what he wanted. Even on the south coast of England, a father's word was law; Robert did not have the physical constitution to disobey regulations and laws. His only means of resistance was his smiling loyalty and the stoical determination to meet his father's expectations, however hard that might be. The boarding school was devoted to preparing its pupils to go on to be cadets, and Con was conspicuous only by his mediocrity, which satisfied everyone, his father, the teachers and his fellow pupils. Then at 13 he went to the Royal Naval College at Dartmouth as a cadet, remaining as he had been before – hard-working but without particular success, pale, someone who kept a low profile and always wore just the right clothes. Scott, who wanted one day to be the first man to reach the South Pole, was really not that different from little Con, who took his first steps towards a naval career at Dartmouth. Then as later, Scott always obeyed orders, like a perfect cog in the declining system of Britain as a world power. He wore his uniform as well as his civilian clothes, in accordance with the rules of the social game – somewhat too neat and tidy. This protective shell masked his lack of decisiveness; in this respect too, Scott and Amundsen were different. Scott wore his rank and position visibly, like the cut of his clothing, to conceal other things, whereas Amundsen's outward appearance was at most a reflection of his mood.

Just like Scott's father in Devonport, Amundsen's father in Christiania hoped that his sons would finish school successfully and go to university. He thought a private school would be suitable for Roald, and from 1881 the boy attended one without particular enthusiasm. He came to take a greater interest in other things, such as the expedition reports of John Franklin, who had set off to find the North-West Passage, the channel between Alaska and Greenland. 'One of his descriptions concerning the desperate retreat of one of his expeditions fascinated me more than anything I had ever read before. He and a few companions had had to struggle for their lives with ice and storms for three terrifying weeks; the only food they had was a few bones they found in an abandoned Indian camp, and before they finally reached the first outposts of civilization they were eventually forced to eat their own leather shoes. It is odd that what most fascinated me about Sir John's story was the description of the privations he and his men had to endure. A strange ambition burned in me to overcome similar sufferings.'

Roald Amundsen, the private schoolboy, wanted to become a Polar explorer, a man of the ice. He was no longer able to talk to his father about this ambition, which was to grow into an obsession; Jens Amundsen died in 1886 at the age of 66 while travelling as a passenger on a steamship somewhere between England and Norway. 'It is hard to lose such a father; but it was God's will, and the will of God must be fulfilled.' The 14-year-old did not want to talk to his mother. When Roald went on about Franklin and other

Polar voyagers, Gustava Amundsen, whose love of the sea had only been love of her husband, dismissed it as youthful daydreaming. To become an adult, he would have to finish school and study medicine, which would be quite enough of an adventure and a voyage of discovery. Amundsen knew that he would never come to anything without the family's blessing; Polar expeditions got through an enormous amount of money. So he immersed himself in the inevitable, but at the same time he prepared for the future as well. In the winter of 1889 he set off with three classmates on a forced march into the mountains to the west of the capital, Christiania, to find out how much pain he could endure. In the early summer, when the whole of Christiania sang the praises of Fridtjof Nansen – who had been the first to cross the frozen interior of Greenland – the die was cast: Amundsen's destiny was set to bind him to the cold.

Yet he was sensible enough to leave school having scraped through his exams and to start studying medicine at the Royal Norwegian Frederick University of Christiania in 1890. This decision brought Amundsen a flat of his own in the city, paid for by his relieved mother, where he had complete freedom to prepare himself for a life outside the realms of middle-class tranquility without losing face with his family. It must have been during this period that Amundsen learned how to adopt a mask, to be obsequious while at the same time getting his own way by doing just that, to make the impossible possible. Studying medicine was just his alibi, and he gritted his teeth and got on with it term after term, right up to September 1893, when he sold a fellow student the skull that had been lying around unregarded in his flat during the three years he had been at university. In that month, Gustava Amundsen had died: Roald Amundsen was free to do what he felt he had to do.

After an appropriate period of mourning, he went on a seven-day-long skiing trip over the Hardangervidda Plateau in the west of Norway together with his brother Leon, who was two years older. It was a dare, a challenge. At times the thermometer fell to minus 40°. Amundsen lived through his first agonies. On his return from this voyage of self-discovery, he tried to get a place on the *Windward*, the ship of the Englishman Frederick George Jackson who was going to sail to Franz Josef Land in the Arctic. But the New Year began with a defeat for Amundsen. Jackson did not hire the ungainly young man, as he needed experienced men, not hot-blooded young adventurers. Amundsen took this calmly. There were other ships sailing north on which he could find a place. In the next two years he went several times to the icy northern sea, as well as to the coasts of Africa; and he read everything that had been written about voyages of discovery, 'all the relevant books I could get my hands on; and so it was I noticed a momentous failure of most of the earlier Polar expeditions. The leaders of these expeditions had not always been ship's captains, so they had almost always had to entrust the running of their ships to experienced seamen. In every such case it had turned out to have disastrous consequences because as soon as the expedition was at sea it no longer

A studio portrait of Captain Robert Falcon Scott taken in the 1890s.

had one leader, but two. This inevitably led to a division of responsibility between the leader of the expedition and the captain, causing constant frictions and differences of opinion. In consequence discipline became slack among the other subordinate members of the expedition. There always ended up being two parties, one consisting of the leader of the expedition and the scientific staff, the other of the captain and his crew. For this reason I was determined not to head an expedition until I was in a position to avoid this mistake. All my efforts were now directed towards gaining the requisite experience in running a ship and training as a captain, so that I would be able to lead my expedition as a sailor as well as an explorer, thus avoiding the formation of two parties.'

When the 21-year-old Amundsen was completing his survival training on the Hardangervidda Plateau, the 25-year-old Scott had already got a good bit of sea-time under his belt, but he still suffered from the seasickness that had exposed him to the teasing of his peers when he was a cadet. The naval port of Dartmouth lived off its glorious past, just as without realizing it the whole of Britain lived with a backward glance to better days. It was from Dartmouth that England's pirates had once sailed the seas, Drake, Morgan and so on, with the blessing of Queen Elizabeth, to make overseas trade more difficult for Spain and Portugal. This was where Elizabeth's fleet had left from in 1588 to destroy the famed Spanish Armada, just as Admiral Nelson was to do two centuries later – Viscount Horatio Nelson, who made England into the greatest naval power, assured British dominance of the Mediterranean and of the Indian subcontinent, and struck down all who sailed against him, French, Spaniards, Danes. But after Nelson the navy froze, as though in awe of its Admiral, who had fallen in 1805 at the battle of Trafalgar. When Scott, over 75 years after Nelson's death, entered Dartmouth College, the guns of the British warships were still muzzle-loaders, as in the days of glory, but the Europeans of the continent were long since equipped with modern breech-loading weapons.

The spirit of Nelson was also present on the *Britannia* when the cadet intake of 1881 moved on to the Royal Navy's school ship – 150 thirteen-year-olds, crammed together below decks. Before experiencing the open seas, they had to go through oppressive overcrowding on board ship: 150 hammocks so closely spaced the boys were practically sleeping on top of one another. As was the case throughout training, everything was subject to the officers' whistles. Discipline, order and cleanliness were the true taskmasters of the College, the aim of which was to incorporate its pupils into a system of blind obedience and rigid hierarchy. These months were both hard and bitter for the young Scott. Regulations determined everything down to the tiniest detail, and the only way of getting on was to play one's part. This Scott did in all respects, but without ever losing his gentle smile, in which he so resembled his mother. He never said anything about Dartmouth, any more than he did about himself; he was always loyal to the Navy, even when he was dying. There were others who were more critical, such as Vice Admiral

Dewar, who wanted to reform naval education and summed up his experiences thus: 'The repressive atmosphere checked initiative and self-confidence. Although the instructional methods were not calculated to stir up the interest or enthusiasm of the cadets, the majority worked hard because their future seniority depended on the result of the passing-out examination. It was not intelligence, character, aptitude for command nor professional zeal that started a young officer on his upward career, but mastery of such subjects as algebra, the binomial theorem or trigonometrical equations.'

In 1883 Scott completed his training with good marks and the rank of midshipman. He had the requisite sense of duty and the equally vital ability to control his emotions. His career followed the usual pattern. After four years at sea he was promoted to sub-lieutenant, then he spent a year at the Greenwich Naval College where he qualified as a full lieutenant. He got a small command, nothing remarkable. Drill, routine work, hoisting the flag, going to receptions; and the rather dull pattern of life at sea. Since the Napoleonic Wars, the Royal Navy had sailed the seas as the symbol of a mighty empire, spick and span, showing the flag, holding the state together. It was jokingly said that the only way to get anywhere in the navy was to make sure your ship had the finest paint job at parades or at the frequently-held regattas; this was called 'promotion by paint'. Scott did not bother about that. In any case, now he did not just receive orders. He was waited on at table, and people stood to attention when he went past. He had now conquered the fear of being sick in front of other people, as he had got the better of his seasickness. Scott was positively glowing with health, and he still had his ever-friendly smile. Others from his year had been promoted before him, perhaps because they had better social connections or the kind of sense of humour in company that got them noticed by their superiors. Still, some people were sure that this conscientious, dapper young man from Plymouth would yet go far, if he were allowed enough time. Others were not convinced; though mediocrity was certainly a guarantee of smooth progress up the ladder of promotion in Her Majesty's navy, it was not exactly a catapult to the top. Scott's constant smile and his blandness definitely stood in the way of rapid progress. So he made his way in the world without really getting anywhere. He got to know the coasts and ports of Peru, Guatemala, Canada and the West Indies, practised obedience and naval discipline, and waited for his next promotion. Sir Clements Markham, at the time still the secretary of the Royal Geographical Society in London, came across Scott when he was participating in a parade in the West Indies. Markham was an eccentric who regarded the navy as the ultimate nursing ground for men; he had left it in his younger years when the cat-o'-nine-tails still reigned supreme on deck because he could not bear the navy's disciplinary regime. He loved young men standing at attention before him in their smart dress uniforms, and he was immediately struck by Robert Scott when he made a public impression by coming first in a regatta. The sailors who took part did not just have to be quick, they had to take down their sails before the finish line, which called upon the discipline of all the sailors taking part. Markham delighted in victorious youth, and tried to get the full measure of them, for he had great plans for them: with their help he wanted to discover the last great continent for Britain, the Antarctic. Clements Markham had joined in an expedition to rescue John Franklin, who had gone missing in 1847 while looking for the North-West Passage and had never been heard of again. He had published several books about explorations and was convinced that only the British navy was capable of penetrating the land around the South Pole. In his view the real problem was getting there in the first place, not reaching the Pole. The navy would be best able to cope with the enormous bodies of water all round the Antarctic. Markham did not seem to have realized that the exploration only really began at the point where ships could reach no further. British sailors would surely be able to deal with a bit of snow, ice and cold. He thought that someone like Scott, whom he had invited to dinner in his cabin, had what it took, the necessary discipline and just enough stubborn endurance; he would cross the ice for Britain. What was he called? – Robert Scott – a name to remember, to file away for the time when Great Britain would send its great expedition to the South Pole.

When Scott sat at Markham's table, he had never yet seen snow, but he had plenty of experience of naval routine. Why should he bother with Markham's bird in the bush when there was already one in his hand? In 1890 a new weapon had been introduced by the navy, the torpedo. The prospects of promotion for those specializing in this modern device would improve, because there was a relative shortage of experienced people. In October 1891 Scott was sent on a torpedo training course which he completed with distinction two years later, having been promoted to torpedo lieutenant; but Scott blotted his copybook. Shortly before the end of the course, he had run a torpedo boat aground when he was placed in command of it during an exercise. The Admiralty's censure was measured: 'Due care does not appear to have been exercised, Scott cautioned to be more attentive in future.' Theory and practice are quite different matters, a lesson that would later be brought home to Scott.

In 1897 John Scott died, having given up 'Outlands', the family home, and taken poorly-paid employment as manager of a Plymouth brewery. Together with her daughters, his widow moved to London and tried without much success to keep their heads above water. A man was needed to take charge of the family. Scott and his elder brother Archibald had to ensure that they did not come to grief, but his brother died in 1898 and now it was up to Scott and his mother's supportive smile. He never complained, but he must have been relieved when Ettie and Rosie, his two older sisters, struck out on their own, Rosie as a nurse in Nigeria, Ettie as an actress, until she agreed to marry William Ellison-Macartney, a Parliamentary Secretary to the Admiralty.

Nonetheless, Scott remained torpedo lieutenant aboard the battleship HMS *Majestic*, the flagship of the Channel

Squadron; he was stuck. His specialist torpedo training had already made him a lieutenant, but he would have liked to be captain on the bridge. He certainly did not mention this to Sir Clements Markham, who had now been elected President of the Royal Geographical Society, when the two men met occasionally in London. They spoke of Markham's favourite topic, the South Pole and its conquest by the Royal Navy. Scott had still never seen snow; it was 1897.

Two years previously, Amundsen had got his master's certificate in Christiania; at the beginning of the next year, he set off on his third excursion into the mountains and glaciers of Norway. In winter, the Norwegian highlands with their snowstorms and biting cold are not dissimilar to the polar regions. He intended to cross the Upper Hardangervidda Plateau with his brother Leon, but the trip was nearly a disaster. The two brothers ended up in a fierce snowstorm without a tent, going round in circles. In the evening they each dug themselves a hole in the snow to provide some shelter from the nighttime cold. At some point, Roald woke up. The ditch had been covered over by a huge snowdrift and he was getting short of air; his sleeping bag was frozen solid, as was his right arm, which he had forgotten to put inside the bag. He was unable to move or cry out, as snowdust clogged his breath. He panicked, which only made things worse. The blood rushed to his head and neck. It took Leon three hours to dig his brother out of the snow, but as soon as he had been rescued he announced that he wanted to go into the ice like Franklin or Nansen, to the North Pole, or at least to pass through the North-West Passage. Leon was the first person in whom Amundsen confided. For many years, Leon would be his most trusted associate, helping to finance his brother's expeditions. In the end, there was a legal dispute between the brothers and Amundsen broke off contact with his brother, referring to him only as his secretary or, if absolutely necessary, by all his forenames. But they were still brothers.

The same year, Amundsen met a man who wanted to sail down the east coast of South America past Cape Horn and make for Graham Land and Victoria Land, the Belgian Adrien de Gerlache. His plan was to winter with four men at Cape Adare, where Borchgrevink had been the first to walk on the Antarctic continent, while his ship, the *Belgica*, went back to Australia. Amundsen was enthusiastic and proposed himself to the leader of the expedition as a participant, as he could demonstrate his experience of the icy northern seas, and he now had a master's certificate. Gerlache liked the young man, who, being Norwegian, knew how to deal with skis, and he signed him up as Second Officer and Second Mate. A salute was fired as the *Belgica* set off on its adventurous journey from Antwerp on 16 August 1897. When she returned to the port on 5 November 1899, Roald Amundsen was years ahead of Scott, though the latter was chronologically his elder by nearly half a decade.

Members of Captain Scott's expedition probing a crevasse.

3

Apprenticeship amidst
Snow and Ice

*'Why, I ask, did we come here? Was it not in order to explore
unknown regions? That is impossible if you stay outside the ice.'*

Roald Amundsen

*'I have a few nebulous ideas, but I am quite prepared to find that
hasty and possibly ill conceived plans must be made on the spot.'*

Robert Falcon Scott

For six decades, ever since James Ross had been the
first man to set eyes on the Great Ice Barrier, the
Antarctic had remained the subject of academic
discussion alone. The Arctic was closer to the world in the
final decade of the 19th century, offering as it did a prof-
itable yield for the fishing industry. Whalers and sealers
traversed the Arctic Ocean in search of easy prey. The hunt
was cold and cruel, and in their home ports the hunters were
admired as hard men. Anything that came in range of their
harpoons was killed, and if these could not reach, the animals
were butchered on the pack ice. In Norway above all, the

hunting of whales and seals was regarded as an education in bravery and manly strength. The newspapers in Christiania or Tromsø did not tire of dressing up the bloody slaughter as a model of national prestige, 'an awesome exercise that may be compared to the great scientific achievements in the Polar regions'. Amundsen too went hunting in order to become familiar with the pack ice and the ships that resisted its pressure. He wrote to his brother: 'The distinctive thing about a sealing ship is its solid construction. Strong wood is necessary, so the sealer is made entirely of oak. In fact that is not quite correct, for the hull of the frame is made of a lighter wood, being surrounded on the outside by the so-called ice shield. The ice shield is made of a layer of oak several feet thick. It encases the inner framework of the hull and is meant to resist the ice pressure, which can be incredibly strong. What distinguishes a sealer is the crow's nest, which is perched under the tip of the main mast. This is the captain's place, where he keeps a lookout for seals and steers the ship through the thick, heavy ice.' He wrote nothing about the hunting itself.

While Amundsen was sailing with the sealer, and Scott was in command of a torpedo boat, the Sixth International Geographical Congress was held in London in 1895. Scientists from all over the world had come to discuss yet again John Franklin's lost expedition to the North-West Passage, and Fridtjof Nansen. In 1893 Nansen had steered a ship, the *Fram*, into the ice to the north of the New Siberian Islands, in order to drift in the pack ice to Spitzbergen, maybe past the

North Pole. This was a risky plan, and its likely success or failure was vigorously debated by the scholars at the Congress. But interest in the South Pole was limited to a few discussions among insiders on the fringes, until the moment when a young man wearing a hired suit surprised the international audience with his casual announcement that he had been the first person to walk on the Antarctic continent, and was making further plans: Carsten Borchgrevink. The Norwegian's tales to the assembled experts about his experiences of Cape Adare and the Ice Barrier made such an impression that the Congress drew up the following resolution: 'The exploration of the Antarctic regions is the greatest piece of geographical exploration still to be undertaken; it should be undertaken before the close of the century.'

This opened up the southern path for future Polar journeys, at the same moment, oddly enough, as Fridtjof Nansen's Polar expedition failed; but no-one in London yet knew about that. As early as March that year, Nansen had left the drifting *Fram* with Hjalmar Johansen in order to advance to the North Pole, kitted out with sledges, dogs and skis. They got further than anyone had before them, up to 84 degrees 14 minutes North, before they had to turn back. They were faced with a 500-mile march back over the pack ice, a long winter, before they were discovered more or less by accident in June 1896 by an British Arctic expedition on the edge of the ice. These were two men who never gave up.

When Nansen and Johansen returned to Norway, where

they were enthusiastically received by their countrymen, the world was already looking southwards, and those attending the London Geographical Congress were enthusiastically setting about organizing expeditions to the Antarctic. The conquest of the South Pole had been twisted into a general assault on a continent, a battle for the South Pole in which each nation wanted to be the first to plant its flag at the Pole; but this general assault started out with a skirmish in the offices of the ministries, a debilitating fight for priority in the allocation of funds to the various projects. Though Sir Clements Markham believed that the impetus of the Congress had brought him within reach of his goal that Britain's flag should be the first to be planted at the Pole, for the time being even his hands remained tied. The navy had other concerns, and was busy with a cautious modernization of its fleet; the British crown looked towards Africa, where war was already stirring in the gold-rich Boer republics. It was only after the turn of the century, when the *Belgica* had returned from the southern sea in defeat, that Britain, like Germany and Sweden, began an Antarctic expedition. Yet even the Belgian naval officer Adrien de Gerlache found the state treasury closed to him when he asked King Leopold II for financial support. The Belgian king could not see the point of conquering an imaginary point on the ice, especially as he was already fully occupied in colonizing the Congo. Unlike Markham, however, de Gerlache was able to interest private sponsors in the idea of raising the Belgian flag on the unknown continent. So he sailed half-way round the Earth,

The Belgica, *a former whaling ship used by Adrien de Gerlache for the Belgian Antarctic expedition in 1896.*

and could be sure of international attention. The whole project was too poorly organized, though, to come to a good end. Amundsen ought to have known better, but after the London Congress he was blinded by his ambition to reach the place at de Gerlache's side that was the centre of world attention.

The crew of the 500-ton former Norwegian whaler was as colourful an assortment as the scientific team. There were Belgians, Norwegians, Poles, a Romanian, and an American doctor. Dr Frederick Cook had already taken part in an expedition to North Greenland, and was later to contest his countryman Peary's claim to have been first to conquer the North Pole. In January 1898, the *Belgica* sighted the first iceberg to the north-west of the South Shetland Islands. Until then the journey had gone without a hitch, apart from a few brawls among the sailors; but all that was about to change.

The leaders of the expedition, the captain and his officers, found it challenging to sail through previously unknown regions; but this terrified the crew all the more when the ship was surprised by a powerful storm between Snow Island and Smith Island, washing a man overboard. With the Belgian flag at half mast, the *Belgica* reached the west coast of Graham Land, a barren piece of land with angular mountains of ice and snow. Fear took root in the berths of the crew.

De Gerlache steered the ship into a channel not recorded on the charts, which were in any case sketchy at best, hoping that it would lead him to the Weddell Sea. What he found was a narrow passage between Graham Land and the Brabant

Islands. Today this passage bears his name, and is regarded as the decisive discovery of the Belgian Antarctic expedition.

Amundsen noted the following about this journey into uncharted waters: 'When I came on deck at midnight, there was a weak storm, heavy, damp snow and thick fog. The lookout I replaced reported that he thought the ship was far away from any land. Nonetheless, I kept a careful watch to forward and leeward. At half past midnight I made out a dark stripe to leeward of the bow; it did not appear to be moving. I did not have long to decide. I threw the tiller to leeward; the ship turned away and left the dark stripe astern. The fog lifted enough for me to make sure of what I thought I had seen: an extensive, high lying area of land, and I am quite sure it was at no great distance. A little earlier or later it would not have been possible to make anything out in the heavy snow and the impenetrable fog. The same thing has happened on several occasions.'

For three weeks the *Belgica* sailed to and fro in the passage, and the two Poles Henryk Arctowski and Anton Dobrowolski went ashore several times to study the geology and the glaciers. Meanwhile, Amundsen tried out his skis on the islands and set off with de Gerlache, Cook, Arctowski and the geophysicist Emile Danco on a one-week sledge tour of Brabant Island, which had just been discovered, to map the De Gerlache Channel from the top of the mountain. He was happy. 'The snow was very loose, so we had to dig out a place for the tent. While three of us got on with this, the other two got the food ready in the lee of the sledge. The first task took the most time. Then our little tent stretched out its tip against the snow and wind. What we needed for the night – sleeping bags and dry socks – was brought into the tent. The rest of the stuff stayed on the sledge, well protected under cover. When the hot pea soup stood before us, wind and snow were forgotten. You couldn't be any happier in a palace. These trips are splendid; I hope I shall have many more opportunities for them.'

In February the sea temperature sank below 1.8° Celsius, and little hexagonal ice crystals began to form on the surface of the water and grow into long needles. The sea was beginning to ice up and the crew became more and more afraid of the inhospitable location. The icy soup became thicker and thicker, forming clumps of ice that rubbed against one another and began to rise up along the edges. The Antarctic winter was on its way. Other captains had withdrawn in the face of the constantly increasing pack ice, but de Gerlache stuck to his ambitious plan of being the first to winter in the Antarctic. He wanted to become a Belgian Nansen, allowing his ship to be frozen in and drift along with the pack ice as far south as possible. This idea found little support even among the scientific crew: he was not suitably equipped, and in any case he had only planned for four men to winter here, while the ship returned with the crew to Australia. Amundsen, who in any case regarded the whole trip as no more than an apprenticeship for his own future projects, wrote: 'Unfortunately, the scientists are showing their fear openly. They are reluctant to go any further into the ice. Why, I ask, did we come here? Was it not in order to explore unknown regions? That is impossible if you stay outside the ice.'

When de Gerlache headed the *Belgica* into the heaving, crashing ice floes on 28 February, his second-in-command must have realized that the captain did not intend to retreat. Two days later, the ship lay amid the ice, locked in for the whole winter. The general disquiet on board led de Gerlache, who did not want to tell the ship's company the truth, or was unable to, to falsify their situation and to announce repeatedly to the crew that he expected them to be released shortly. At some point the crew accepted their fate, to be the first to live through a southern Polar winter, the time of darkness when the sun does not rise for months on end, the cold, and the consuming feeling of isolation, day in, day out, month after month. No-one could predict whether they would ever get out of the ice again, or whether the *Belgica* would end up being squashed by it like a cardboard box. Two of the sailors went mad, and others fell victim to scurvy, a disease caused by acute vitamin C deficiency.

The ship's doctor, Dr Cook from Boston, did not know anything about the causes of scurvy; until 1900, more sailors had fallen victim to it than were killed in sea battles. But he thought he knew of a cure for this terrible disease, which makes the flesh rot. De Gerlache, however, rejected the idea of making raw seal or penguin meat the main food on his ship; after all, he had plenty of tinned food on board. The results were the same as they had always been over the centuries when lack of fresh food led to the body receiving insufficient Vitamin C: swollen limbs, bleeding gums, loose teeth, lethargy to the point of mental confusion, and depression. The crew grew more apathetic. Emile Danco, who had paid a lot of money for his place on board the *Belgica*, died. Few paid any attention to Dr Cook, but Amundsen had no objection to chewing raw, blubbery-tasting meat. He never permitted himself to become infected by the general low spirits. 'Tomorrow the sun will reach the end of its northward journey and start to make its way back. Of course I am looking forward to seeing it again, but I haven't missed it for a moment. On the contrary, this is just how I wanted it ... I hope I have the health and strength to continue the task I have begun.'

When the sun climbed back over the horizon, the first Antarctic winter to be lived through by Europeans was over; the raw meat was accepted as medicine by more and more of the ship's company, if not as food. Hope returned and plans were made; but the *Belgica* was still immobile. Once again there was a quarrel, this time between the captain and Amundsen, his second officer. 'I attached myself to you without asking for payment; it was a question of honour, not money. You have insulted this honour by denying me my right. As far as I am concerned, there is no longer a Belgian Antarctic expedition, and the *Belgica* is just an ordinary ship locked in the ice. It is my duty to help the men on board. For this reason, captain, I will continue my work as if nothing had happened.' What had happened?

Before the expedition departed, de Gerlache had had

to promise the Belgian Geographical Society that Belgian officers would be given preference should the command have to be passed on, whatever their rank. After the first mate, it would not be Amundsen, the second mate, but the third, Maierts, a Belgian. The first mate remained at his post, but when Amundsen discovered this arrangement, which he saw as scornful of his abilities, he reacted in accordance with his passionate character. In subsequent years, his reaction to criticism or doubts about him, on whatever grounds, would have an almost pathological intensity. He was not the sort of man to allow others to judge him; he could not stand criticism. When he was exposed to it, he believed to an almost hysterical degree that he was the victim of jealous persecution. But now he had to put up with this imagined degradation, for the *Belgica* was still frozen in the ice, and had been for nine months.

In January 1899 the men began to saw a canal through the ice, also using explosives, as they had discovered a water channel a mile from the ship that had remained open the whole winter. if they could reach it, the *Belgica* would be saved. But the narrow, painstakingly-cut passage kept closing up under the pressure of the ice. Everyone was terrified by the prospect of having to spend a second winter there, and they were entertaining the idea of abandoning the ship and making their way over the ice by sledge to the land. On 15 February at two in the morning, the canal opened for a moment. The engine was fired up, and the *Belgica* finally set slowly off under its own steam. For a month it made its way tortuously through the 700-metre long canal; at times, hope of reaching the open see faded. 'We are making no progress, we are utterly lost … The engineer comes on deck. He can see the situation with his own eyes. There is no need to ask him to keep the power up. In a trice he is below decks again, and the engine chugs away as never before, and never again. We struggle forwards, inch by inch, foot by foot, yard by yard. We are saved. At the critical point, the ice gave way. That was the end of the first winter spent in the Antarctic.'

On 14 March, the ship was finally free. Just 14 days later, on 27 March, they dropped anchor in Punta Arenas, the Chilean port in the Straits of Magellan; then the *Belgica* made its way home to Antwerp across the Atlantic. Roald Amundsen was so deeply annoyed with de Gerlache that he left the ship at Punta Arenas and returned to Norway on a post ship. He had set out to gather experience and test his abilities in the Antarctic night, and now he had no further interest in the expedition. De Gerlache and Cook published books about their experiences, but Amundsen remained silent, apart from making an offer to Fridtjof Nansen. 'Professor Nansen, I have just got back from the Belgian Antarctic expedition, and I make so bold as to enquire whether you would have any interest in hearing something of the journey. If you are, I am at your disposal.'

Amundsen never mentioned Adrien de Gerlache again, but Dobrowolski, another member of the expedition, wrote in enthusiastic tones about the Belgian and the results of their Antarctic journey. 'The expedition returned home with the first complete meteorological record of a whole year, the foundation of an Antarctic climatology, the first proof of a ring of low pressure around the anticyclone of the Antarctic continent, as well as the first collection of ocean organisms from the Antarctic over the course of a full year ... Finally, our sea journey was the apprenticeship of that unusual explorer, the Napoleon of the polar regions, Amundsen.' Amundsen, however, was not particularly interested in meteorological records or the foundations of Antarctic climatology. He was not even interested in the Antarctic, since his plans all involved the Arctic, as was traditional; that was where he wanted to achieve his victories, to the north, for himself, for his country. To reach the North Pole, to be better than Nansen, was his sole aim in life. That was why Amundsen's years on the *Belgica* were years of apprenticeship that would spur on his imagination. The southern continent was not important to him – not yet.

Silently and without attracting public attention, he returned to Christiania, a private citizen who had undertaken a scientific journey and wanted to recover from his exertions. Like many people at that time, Amundsen was waiting for the turn of the century; he did his military service and cycled through western Europe with his brother Leon. He had seen enough snow for the time being, and he showed little concern that other nations were preparing exploratory journeys to the Antarctic, as was Amundsen's childhood playmate Carsten Borchgrevink, who put together his own Antarctic expedition with £35,000 from an English publisher, who expected to do well out of the deal. In the spring of 1899, Borch-grevink sailed the *Southern Cross* to Cape Adare, where he built the first research station on the Antarctic continent; in this hut he and nine companions survived the first winter spent on dry land. Let Borchgrevink do well in the Antarctic; Amundsen wanted the North Pole.

Sir Clements Markham, who felt Borchgrevink's British-Norwegian expedition was a national humiliation, as the only British share in the enterprise had been the financing, detected a slight hope on the horizon for his plans in the final days of the 19th century. A London businessman promised to give £25,000 towards a purely British expedi-tion. This meant that there was £40,000 in the kitty, and in the summer of 1899 the First Lord of the Treasury raised the prospect of a further £45,000 grant from Parliament, with a £5,000 contribution from the Royal Geographical Society. Queen Victoria wished the expedition well, and the Prince of Wales became its patron. This sudden generosity was the political reaction to the intention of Kaiser Wilhelm II to raise the German flag in the Antarctic through an expedition under the command of Erich von Drygalski. The Reichstag in Berlin had already approved the necessary funds, and the royal family did not want to give up the Antarctic region to this rival without a fight, as Germany's aggressive trade policy and growing military strength were a threat to British interests.

Scott, who had been a lieutenant for ten years and had no prospects of climbing further up the career ladder, knew that it might help matters if he put himself forward for a prominent role in the South Pole project. Thus it was that, shortly after the Antarctic expedition had been announced, he appeared in Markham's flat in Eccleston Square and offered to be the leader of the expedition. Markham had other men in mind, but they refused him. The navy was preparing for a showdown with Germany, so nobody wanted to be sent out to this far-off corner of the world where scientific laurels could perhaps be won, but no military ones. Markham, nearly 70, and the 31-year-old lieutenant of the new torpedo arm came to an agreement. A few months later, on 30 June 1900, Scott was promoted to Commander and officially named as the leader of the National Antarctic Expedition, with £90,000 at its disposal – over £2 million in today's money.

Scott was certainly a compromise candidate, and nobody was quite sure if he had what it would take, not even Markham. But the President of the Royal Geographical Society did not really have any other choice, as time was short. Scott, on the other hand, had his promotion in his pocket, and double the pay; he had to accept that Sir Clements was preparing for the expedition, while its commander merely stood at attention. Markham remained a force to be reckoned with despite his eccentricities, a typical figure of Queen Victoria's reign, who did not look beyond British shores. He had the ship built in Dundee, even though Britain could no longer build large wooden ships. When the *Discovery* set off on its journey, it had several leaks, and had to be repaired *en route*.

Even more important for Scott's future was Markham's

entrenched opposition to using dogs as to pull sleds. 'Dogs are useful to Greenland Eskimos and Siberians. In recent times much reliance has been placed upon dogs for Arctic travelling. Yet nothing has been done with them compared to what men have achieved without dogs.' British sailors had no need of dogs, nor of skis. 'I have been accustomed to ski since 1877, but should never think of using them if I had to drag anything after me – that would be well nigh an impossibility – or of wearing them on firm snow, for which they are not suited.' Like the United Kingdom generally in the time of Queen Victoria, Markham was stuck in a rigid position. Scott stood next to him smiling. He knew no better, never yet having seen the snow.

In the autumn of 1900 he visited Nansen in Christiania – a duty call to receive the blessing of the man who had so famously crossed Greenland and led the *Fram* expedition. Nansen, a doctor of zoology and regarded as an international expert, did manage to persuade Scott to take at least a few dogs and skis on his journey. Scott never got the hang of either dogs or skis. Later, on board the *Discovery* in Cowes, he read the letter Nansen gave him. 'You are inaugurating a new period in Antarctic exploration. I am certain that you will have the time and opportunity to make great discoveries in southern waters, for every depth measurement and every water sample is a new conquest for science. The best parting words I can find are those used by the eskimos: May you always sail in open waters!'

In January 1901 Queen Victoria died, and Edward VII

ascended the throne. The King inspected the *Discovery* and its crew before the ship left Cowes and sailed out of the Solent into the Channel. Every occasion has its rituals, and no national mission is complete without the blessing of the country. On the 26th, his ship entered the Atlantic. Two weeks later he had the picture of Sir Clements removed from the wall of the officers' mess; it was his crew, his expedition to the cold, whereas the President of the Royal Geographical Society in London was sitting in the warmth and waiting for other people to pull his chestnuts out of the fire for him. Scott was burning with ambition.

On 18 January 1902 he saw the Antarctic for the first time, like most of those on board the *Discovery*. He wrote to Nansen: 'The expedition has a crew with little knowledge and no experience except such as pertains to the sea and its moods. Moreover I am distinctly conscious of a want of plan. I have a few nebulous ideas, but I am quite prepared to find that hasty and possibly ill conceived plans must be made on the spot.'

After the *Discovery* had anchored briefly at Cape Adare, Scott steered the ship beyond the coast of Victoria Land further southwards to the McMurdo Sound and eastwards along the Ice Barrier. Like Borchgrevink two years before, he reached the Bay of Whales and sailed further east. On 30 January 1902 he discovered previously unknown land at the eastern end of the Ross Barrier; he named it King Edward VII Land. Logbook entry: '4.30 p.m. Stood into a bay Hills plainly seen inland. 5.50. Observed land over ice cap. 6.45.

Observed bare rock projecting through snow capped hills.'
Pack ice prevented their going further, but *Discovery* was able
to escape its clutches at the last minute. Scott allowed the
crew a two-day rest in the Bay of Whales. For many of them,
this was their first encounter with ice and snow. They tried
the skis and sent up a hydrogen balloon to a height of 244
metres. Scott must have been impressed by what he saw from
the observation basket: a gently rising ice shelf, a wasteland
glittering in the sun all the way to the great mountains in
the south.

Scott did not trust the ice formation. Borchgrevink had
spoken of a straight run to the South Pole, but he would
not anchor his ship here; the ice floes rose up far too close
to the *Discovery*. Nine years later, Amundsen set up the base
camp for his assault on the Pole amidst the same dangers,
but Scott turned back at the western end of the great ice
fragment towards the McMurdo Sound, recommended to
him by the librarian of the Royal Geographical Society as the
best starting-point for the exploration of the interior of the
Antarctic continent. Below Mount Erebus, where the Sound
gives into the open Ross Sea, Scott found a shallow spot,
his winter harbour, protected on almost all sides against ice
pressure. He had reached his immediate goal, but discipline
on board remained strict.

During the crossing of the Ross Barrier a sailor wrote
in his diary: '… this monotonous scrubbing of decks every
morning in the Antarctic at temperatures far below freezing
is absolutely awful. It is as if they were incapable of forget-

ting the naval order – thou shalt scrub the decks without fail, whatever the conditions may be.' The maintenance of discipline and the execution of orders once given were the first commandment of the Royal Navy. Scott would eventually curse this commandment – but only in private.

It was Markham's idea for a small landing party to overwinter in the three tiny huts while the ship returned to Australia. Scott decided against this, allowing the 485-ton *Discovery*, 52.5 metres long and 10.5 metres wide, to freeze in as the waters below Mount Erebus began to ice over. The halyards, the rudder and the screw were removed, the boiler was drained and the decks were covered with tarpaulins.

On 23 April the Polar night descended on the crew for more than a hundred days. Scott himself remained in the captain's cabin on board the *Discovery*; when he got cold, he stuck his feet in a box of hay from the Arctic. He disliked furs. The expedition ship was at 78 degrees South, 500 miles nearer to the Pole than all previous winter quarters. The Germans under Drygalski were far to the north at the edge of the Antarctic circle before Kaiser Wilhelm II Land, as were the Swedes under Nordenskjöld on Snow Hill Island in the Weddell Sea. The British expedition had the longest Antarctic night ahead of them.

As on the *Belgica*, long darkness, solitude and temperatures below minus 50° spread despair among the crew of the *Discovery*, as well as the fear that they would never get free of the ice. Scott reacted with unchanging friendliness, a permanent smile and the traditional separation between officers and men. He inspected the rations and held divine service every Sunday, followed by the inevitable roast mutton. He was subsequently criticized for the fact that two crewmen had been taken just as officers' servants. Even in the snow, the discipline of the Victorian navy was preserved, perhaps because Scott believed that keeping rigidly to a daily routine would provide a psychological bulwark against the extreme pressure. But ice, snow and cold pay no attention to the preservation of discipline, and so Scott tried to keep up the morale of his team by providing distractions. At midday, when the moon lit up the ice, they played football. After supper the scientists and officers had discussion sessions, and amateur theatricals were produced with equipment brought specially from England to cheer up the rest of the crew. Ernest Shackleton, an officer of the Merchant Navy and a connoisseur of lyric poetry, in the Antarctic for the first time like Scott, also produced a monthly magazine, the *South Polar Times*, in which anyone could publish articles. The bitterness that was later to arise between the two men started out during this polar night as friendship; Shackleton was popular with the men on board the *Discovery*, whereas Scott kept his distance. Scott mistrusted Shackleton, but he admired the stocky junior officer Edward Evans, a practical man, physically strong and still calm even in awkward situations – just the right sort of man for the ice. More than anyone else, Scott was friendly with Dr Edward Wilson, who had been accepted on to the *Discovery* as a civilian; Wilson was the first man he told of his plan to march to the South Pole once the winter was over.

On 22 August 1902 the sun rose above the horizon again, and Scott sent out several land expeditions for initial reconnaissance. Food depots were established and marked with flags. Their radius of action increased, but with it the difficulties to which they were exposed. To get up on the shelf ice, the sledges had to be raised on rollers secured to rods hammered into the ice. On 2 November, in good weather, Scott, Wilson and Shackleton received a lively send-off from the whole crew. The first advance into *terra incognita* began with 19 dogs harnessed to a single leading rope before five sledges. Scott knew no better, and the three men had difficulty getting the team to pull. Huskies draw differently from oxen or horses; because they are not equally disciplined, they love bursts of speed and frequent rests. They are not suited to the evenly-paced trot of British persistence. The men could not deal with the dogs, and nobody knew that the animals needed a leader to be chased after by the pack. The other problem was attached to their feet: skis. Scott, Wilson and Shackleton were not skiers, and the boards were continually slipping away under their feet, until they threw the skis onto the sledges and marched laboriously over hard or loose snow behind the dog team. Their canvas jackets, the navy's standard clothing, were too tight in the wrong places, offering insufficient protection against the cold. Wilson went snow-blind for a time, Shackleton fell ill with scurvy, and the huskies got sick. The animals had been fed on biscuit through the winter; only when the sledge journey began were they given salt cod brought from England. For 18 months the dogfood had lain untended in *Discovery*'s hold; now it had gone off, and the huskies got diarrhoea and became thin, many of them dying. Those that died were fed to the living. Yet still, on 25 November 1902 Scott, Shackleton and Wilson reached 82 degrees 17 minutes South; they had come within 620 kilometres of the Pole, further than any man so far.

The return journey was murderous. The dogs would no longer allow themselves to be put in harness in front of the sledges, so the men pulled them themselves. For two days Scott wore himself out in this way before ordering Wilson to kill the two remaining dogs. Shackleton collapsed and refused to be pulled on a sledge by the other two. Wilson and Scott also suffered from scurvy; their limbs were swollen and their joints ached.

On 3 February Scott, Wilson and Shackleton returned to the base camp in the McMurdo Sound, where the *Discovery* remained frozen into the ice. The crew gave them a reception as hearty as the sendoff they had been given three months before, and took lots of photographs of them. Wilson noted in his diary: 'We must have been worth photographing, I began to realise then how filthy we were – long sooty hair, black greasy clothes … noses all peeling, and sore, lips all raw, everything either sunburnt or bleached …'

Shackleton, hauled aboard by helpful hands, remained in a critical condition, and Scott sent him back to England with the *Morning*, the relief ship that was tied up on the edge of the pack ice in the open Ross Sea. Shackleton wanted to stay, but he had to set off for home. In this way the friendship between the two men came to an end before it had begun. Thinking of other men who were sent back, but also of Shackleton, Scott wrote to Markham: 'It was a mistake to try and mix the merchant service & Naval element ... they have never pulled well together.'

The *Morning* had been sent to the Antarctic by Markham to bring Scott an official order to return, but an unofficial letter from Markham urged him to remain, which fitted in with the commander's plan; at 35 years old, he had discovered a taste for snow. In addition, the *Discovery* remained frozen into McMurdo Sound the whole summer long, so that there was no way to avoid passing a second winter there. The following spring, Scott embarked on a second great exploratory journey with just a few men, 600 miles to the west in Victoria Land, going up the Ferrar Glacier; a debilitating upward march with no dogs. The sledges were drawn by the men for nine to ten hours each day, a burden of 240 pounds – up the glacier. Scott proved to be strong as a bear, and drove his band ever onwards. One man wrote in his diary: 'It's really too bad for anything, I can't agree with forcing men to such work, all the time one is at the highest strain, & it is that, that I don't like to see, – something might snap.' Once they had arrived at the high plateau, Scott sent all but two of the men back. With Edward Evans and William Lashley, Leading Stoker, he continued, before turning back at 146 degrees 33 minutes West. 'The circumstances were hard, I cannot find anything in polar history to equal them. I am proud of my polar journey though as long as I live I never want to revisit the summit of Victoria Land. The conditions were so bad that three of my people couldn't stick it – and were sent back.' Scott was happy.

At the beginning of 1904, the ice situation in McMurdo Sound remained hopeless, showing no sign of improvement. The pack ice towered up metres high. This time two ships, the *Morning* and the *Terra Nova*, approached the trapped crew to relieve them. The orders from London were unambiguous: 'If the *Discovery* cannot be got out of the ice, you will abandon her and bring your people back in the relief ships as My Lords cannot under existing circumstances consent to the further employment of officers and men of the Royal Navy in the Antarctic.' Like de Gerlache off Graham Land, Scott broke through the ice with explosives, reaching open water at the last minute.

On 1 April 1904, Scott arrived at Lyttelton, where he received a telegram from the Admiralty: 'Admiralty congratulates your safe return.' King Edward VII cabled: 'I congratulate you and your gallant crew on your splendid achievements, and I hope to see you all on your return to England.' On 10 September the *Discovery* anchored in Portsmouth, and Scott was promoted to Captain.

As a Polar explorer, the best was behind him, but he thought everything was to come. He had found the central task of his life, to complete his unfinished business by chasing after an imaginary line in the snow. Just as Amundsen wanted to conquer the North Pole, Scott wanted the South. He had been 620 kilometres short of it. He had set off on the march ill-prepared, with insufficient experience of snow and cold, of the logistical preparations needed for such a forced march, and how to manage dogs and skis. If those three men had marched beyond 82 degrees South, it would certainly not just have been huskies that died from profound exhaustion, tormenting hunger and crippling cold. Scott was obsessed enough with the Pole to have exceeded his limits on 30 December 1902; only Shackleton's collapse had saved him and Wilson.

In London, Scott at first withdrew from public gaze to spend time with Sir Clements Markham, to fulfil his final duty as leader of the *Discovery* expedition. He wrote the expected account of the journey, which appeared in 1905 under the title *The Voyage of the Discovery* and was a great success. Those who had actually been on the trip reacted with reserve to their commander's gifts as a writer; he knew how to combine fact and fiction. Shackleton in particular – who was now preparing for his own expedition to the South Pole – saw himself described as a weakling, but he managed to get Scott to publicly revise many of his statements.

So it was that the competition for the Pole began as a struggle between Englishmen in the back rooms of the Royal Geographical Society. 'I am astonished,' Scott wrote when he heard the news of Shackleton's plans, 'I am in doubt as to the spirit in which Shackleton has acted – it may be coincidence but it looks as though he has had an inkling of my intentions & has rushed to be first in the field. Shackleton owes everything to me. I got him into the Expedition – I had him sent home for his health. I did much for him.' For both of them, the whole thing had become a question of masculine honour, or what passed for it at the beginning of the 20th century. Scott wanted to restore his lost honour, Scott to maintain his own; both wanted to be the first one to complete the journey to the Pole. 'I hold it would not have been playing the game for anyone to propose an expedition to McMurdo Sound until he had ascertained that I had given up the idea of going again – and I think I am justified in a stronger view when steps of this sort are taken by one of my own people without a word to me.' The third man, Wilson, became involved in this dispute too; he wrote to Shackleton, 'if you go to McMurdo Sound & even reach the Pole – the gilt will be off the gingerbread because of the insinuation which will almost certainly appear in the minds of a good many, that you forestalled Scott who had a prior claim to the use of that base'.

On the eve of the First World War, Britain, like the whole of Europe, had need of heroes – but heroes who kept to the rules of the game, who might even go heroically to their deaths, always in a spirit of fair play. Shackleton was such a man. Despite the gulf separating the two men, he wrote to Scott: 'Since the base at McMurdo Sound was discovered by you and as my plans cut across yours, you asked me to change my base. This I agreed to do. I am leaving the McMurdo Sound base to you, and will land either at the Barrier Inlet or at King Edward VII Land, whichever is the most suitable.' Did sportsmanship lie behind this declaration, in the spirit of mountaineers who will not climb to a peak along a new route begun by another climber, but not completed? Or was it that Shackleton did not want his intended victory over Scott to be diminished by following in his footsteps to attain it? It amounts to much the same thing, and in any case, the shortest route to the Pole, beyond the Ross Sea, awaited whoever could conquer it. Shackleton set off for the Antarctic on 7 August 1907 in the *Nimrod*, a small Newfoundland whaler. Scott remained behind and had to wait and see what Shackleton would leave for him – defeat, or the glory of reaching the hotly-contested Pole first.

At this point Amundsen, Scott's actual competitor, was being given a hero's welcome after passing through the North-West Passage for the first time in the *Gjøa*. Scott too was happy to recognize Amundsen's achievement; he felt linked to him by their joint passion for conquering the poles of the Earth – Amundsen the North Pole, Scott the South Pole.

But Amundsen was very far from being a sportsman in the British mould.

A balloon being deflated close to the Discovery *after an attempted ascent during Captain Scott's first expedition to the Antarctic in 1902.*

4

The Gauntlet or,
An Ace up One's Sleeve

*'It was the power of the unknown over the human spirit that
drove men into the Polar regions. It drives us to the hidden
powers and secrets of nature, down into the immeasurably small
microscopic world and also out into the unexplored regions of
the universe. It will leave us no peace until we know the planet
on which we live from the uttermost depths of the ocean to the
topmost layers of the atmosphere.'*

Fridtjof Nansen

*'We were very near to the magnetic pole – both the old one and
the new one – and we probably went past both of them. But our
trip was certainly no great success.'*

Roald Amundsen

Ever since Christopher Columbus had landed on the eastern coast of Central America in 1492, thereby discovering a huge new continent, Europe's sailors had been looking for a maritime passage to enable a landing on the west coast of America. In 1520 Magellan discovered El

Paso, the passage from the southern Atlantic into the Pacific. Because contemporary geographers could only conceive of the division of water and land as being symmetrical, they were all convinced that the Straits of Magellan must have an equivalent in the north of the New World. Many explorers set off through the unknown Arctic labyrinth of islands, to discover the North-West Passage, but the inhospitable conditions of the frozen Arctic sea stopped them all.

As a schoolboy, Amundsen had read the reports of all these expeditions with enthusiasm, and his imagination had been fired by the fate of John Franklin, who had disappeared in the Passage without trace in 1845 with the ships *Erebus* and *Terror*, together with his crew of 159 men. Like Franklin, he wanted to travel into the Polar night, suffer like him, test his character in unknown terrain, and return home as a hero. The North-West Passage had still not been found, and Amundsen decided to turn his dream into a reality. After he had received his master's certificate, allowing him to command a ship outside Norwegian waters, he sought out Georg Neumayer, the Director of the Deutsche Seewarte in Hamburg and an authority on terrestrial magnetism. Neumayer spent 40 days explaining to Amundsen how to use various items of equipment and how to calculate the position of the magnetic poles. Every expedition had to have an official motive, as Amundsen knew, a scientific basis. The desire of a young, still unknown man for heroic deeds would not be enough to raise sufficient capital to carry out the plan. At the turn of the century, geophysicists were still divided as to whether the magnetic poles of the Earth were mobile or fixed. In 1831 James Clark Ross, searching for the North-West Passage, had found the Magnetic North Pole and measured its position; if his measurement were repeated, the dispute would be settled. Neumayer greeted Amundsen's plan with enthusiasm. 'Today told Prof. N. of my plan to determine the present position of the Magnetic North Pole. Prof. N. thought this would be of great scientific significance.'

Now Fridtjof Nansen too had to be convinced; there was no getting round it. Anyone who planned polar ventures required the famous man's blessing. Along with the writers Ibsen, Bjørnson and Hamsun, the painter Munch and the composer Grieg, Nansen was one of the few Norwegians of international significance. His spectacular journeys through Greenland and the drift with the *Fram* had made him world famous, not just among geographers. Nansen was working for the separation of Norway from Sweden, and was widely respected abroad as an advocate of an independent Norway. He was one of the founders of the League of Nations, and later its High Commissioner for Refugees. In 1918 he urged the repatriation of German soldiers from the Soviet Union; his idea of a League of Nations passport, the so-called Nansen passport, for the stateless, refugees, emigrants, Armenians, Chaldaeans and Saarlanders was recognized by 31 states. When Amundsen paid court to Nansen, respectfully and in a starched collar, his experiences on the *Belgica* aroused the professor's attention. Did Amundsen know that Nansen was planning an Antarctic expedition of his own with the *Fram*? Just as much as Neumayer, Nansen was impressed by Amundsen's plan, and gave the young man all the support he could.

Against the wishes of his brothers, Amundsen used his inheritance to buy a strong seaworthy wooden sloop, the *Gjøa*, and had her overhauled; new ice sheathing was fitted and a paraffin motor installed. That was the end of his money, but more was needed to fit the ship out satisfactorily. Nansen appealed to Oskar II, the King of Sweden and Norway. 'Amundsen inspires trust, he has unusually strong capabilities, both as organizer and as leader of an Arctic expedition. If Your Majesty is kind enough to support the project with a gift, I believe this would help Amundsen twice over; for in addition to the financial support itself, Your Majesty's example would make it relatively easy to get money from rich men.' King Oskar reacted immediately with a donation of 10,000 kroner – a political calculation, as he did not want to give up Norway, but Nansen was spokesman of the national independence movement. As the King gave, so did his subjects; Amundsen was able to assemble his crew and complete his preparations. The world soon learned what his plan was: 'I will set off in the *Gjøa* in spring 1903, with seven men on board in total. My preference for a small ship like this one is because the waters we shall sail in are often shallow and narrow. In such circumstances the important thing is to have a vessel of small draft that can be manoeuvred in a tight corner. A simple boat, especially one built for fishing, needs fewer men and is consequently also cheaper to equip.'

It took more time than he thought, and money became tight again. Some of his creditors who had advanced capital to the expedition wanted to take their deposits out of the project, since this North-West Passage business seemed risky. When Amundsen declared himself bankrupt, they threatened to impound his ship. During the night of 17 June 1903, the *Gjøa* secretly left the port of Christiania, and when the Norwegian coast disappeared behind the horizon, Amundsen cracked open a bottle of rum. 'Now, lads, we are free of the creditors. Now everything depends on every man doing his duty. That's easy. Cheers and bon voyage!' He did not tell the crew that the shipowner Olaf Ditlev-Simonsen, a distant relative, had got him out of difficulty before the departure with another 10,000 kroner.

He was 31 when he passed the west coast of Greenland and sailed into northern Canada's labyrinth of islands in search of a passage, and 34 when the *Gjøa* was received back in Norway's capital as warmly as Fridtjof Nansen had been. Amundsen had succeeded in being the first to traverse the long-sought North-West Passage, and received a hero's welcome from a little country that had just freed itself from Swedish tutelage. The tone of the speeches with which he was received was correspondingly heartfelt: 'While we here at home were involved in the political struggle to attain the position we thought we deserved in the international community, a poor band of men struggled for the same goal on board a little skiff high up in the eternal ice and snow – to show the world that the Norwegian people does possess the culture and discipline, the power of self-sacrifice, that give us the right to exist as a free nation.'

On 26 October 1905, King Oskar II of Sweden was forced to bow to the result of a referendum and abolish the union of Sweden and Norway, which had existed since 1814. In a second referendum, the independent Norwegians voted for a constitutional monarchy as the future form of the state, placing the Danish Prince Carl on the throne as Haakon VII. In a time of such political upheavals, the country saw Amundsen's successful expedition as the embodiment of the nation's image of itself. Nansen, who had now been sent to Britain as the ambassador of independent Norway, played down the national feeling of his countrymen before the Royal Geographical Society in London. After Amundsen had reported to the committee on the results of the expedition, Nansen said: 'As Captain Amundsen has just pointed out, it is thanks to the preceding efforts of British sailors that he was able to perform this great deed. But it was a Norwegian who was lucky enough to bring the search for the North-West Passage to its conclusion. I believe that we may say that we belong to the same breed, and we all have the same bold heart. Time and fate may weaken it, but its will to strive, to search, to find, and never to give up, is a strong one.'

Heroic deeds were in demand on the eve of the First World War, and emotional words came easily to every-one's lips. Norwegians, Germans and Englishmen spoke equally of national honour and of the fatherland's need for men prepared to devote themselves to their country, to the point of self-sacrifice if need be. Scott too was schooled in this spirit, and he and his countrymen would later use such language to glorify his second expedition to the South Pole when it ended in catastrophe.

Amundsen on the other hand was made of different stuff, his responsibility being only to himself. When necessary he knew how to turn out in his Sunday best, but none of that could conceal his strong sense of his own worth, his independence from social conventions, which he always knew how to make use of when they did not stand in his way. When it came to financing his plans, he was a past master at putting on a modest face and flattering donors. So he was no rebel, but he was a coldly calculating strategist. The journey through the North-West Passage was his first masterpiece.

He had hired the best people, men with experience of the Polar sea, not scientists. Amundsen had prepared thoroughly for this trip, acquiring a basic knowledge of geophysics – enough, in any case, to allow him to claim scientific validity for the expedition and to attract donors. In reality, his interest in measuring the location of the magnetic North Pole was marginal; he wanted to gain experience and test out survival strategies that would permit him to be the first to conquer the North Pole. When difficulties arising from the weather had forced him to abandon the exact measurement of the magnetic pole, he had been positively relieved. 'We were very near to the magnetic pole – both the old one and the new one – and we probably went past both of them. But our trip was certainly no great success.' Rather than making good this failure, he preferred to winter with an Eskimo family who taught him and his men their ways, and how to survive in the Polar region. 'In the morning we built igloos. Within three hours we had completed two splendid igloos in our two pairs. We need more practice. We'll get it later. The actual building is not difficult.' He learned how to manage dogs, the advantages of wearing furs and how to ice up the runners of a sledge to make it go more smoothly. Here, in the northernmost regions of North America, was Amundsen's real school in the ways of the ice and the cold, and his teachers were the land's aboriginal inhabitants, people who were still almost living in the Stone Age, at least from the point of view of Europeans. Amundsen was friendly to them because he desired knowledge. 'My greatest hope for my friends the Netsilik Eskimos is that civilization may never approach them,' he wrote, yet he tried to teach them table manners. Years later he took two Chukchen girls from their tribe to Norway; he said he had saved them, and sent them to school and clothed them in the latest fashions. He took them for walks as he took his dogs, answering the talk this caused with a frosty smile – for a while. Then when he had money troubles once more, he sent the two girls back. No-one knows what became of them.

When Amundsen had returned to Norway after his successful transit of the Passage (which had no use as a maritime route) he answered a reporter's question about future expeditions as follows: 'The destination this time will not be the Arctic Sea, but the unexplored icy wastes of the Antarctic.' He had travelled more than 1,500 kilometres through the Polar landscape on snowshoes or with dog teams, had let his ship ice in, and had learned to build igloos; he felt strong enough to confront the Antarctic. He wanted to discover the magnetic South Pole, which would be the final training, the prelude to the actual, great goal: the conquest of the North Pole. Possibly Amundsen did not just want to conquer the magnetic South Pole, but the geographic South Pole itself. He agreed with Nansen that the Antarctic landscape would be a smooth run for skis and for Greenland dogs.

Amundsen thus laid claim to territory on which others believed they had a prior claim, namely Britain and Fridtjof Nansen. From Nansen he wanted a ship, the *Fram*, and from the world-renowned Royal Geographical Society its blessing as a Polar explorer. What was more, Ernest Shackleton had already initiated the contest for the South Pole with an advert in a London daily paper. 'Men sought for dangerous journey – low pay, biting cold, long months of complete darkness, constant danger. Safe return uncertain.'

Over 400 had responded; Shackleton took 15 of them, including Frank Wild, a descendent of James Cook. On 7 August the little group set off from Cowes on board the former sealer *Nimrod*, after a visit on board from the King. Shackleton had financed the expedition with £20,000 from his own funds, with advances from newspapers and publishers who intended to publish his reports, and a bank loan.

Amundsen, who had attentively followed the preparations for the Shackleton expedition, thought he had been robbed of half his chance to reach the South Pole first. Like Scott, his hands were now tied for the time being, and he had to await the outcome of the voyage of the *Nimrod*. He thought Shackleton was probably unlikely to reach the Pole with nine sledge dogs and a handful of Siberian ponies, especially as the British team were no skiers. But he was worried about Shackleton's specially modified tracked car, which should be well suited to the snow, and save the strength of the men. He could certainly hope that it would not work, but he did not know this for certain. If Shackleton did reach the South Pole, he would still have the other end of the Earth, the North Pole. If Shackleton failed, Amundsen would have to have completed his preparations in order to be ready to go before the next great British expedition, which would probably set off for the Antarctic under Scott in 1910. That much he knew, because the Royal Geographical Society in London made no secret of its plans.

Whether North Pole or South, all his plans were initially frustrated by the simple fact that he had no ship in which to undertake a Polar assault. He had used his own fortune for the *Gjøa* and borrowed money for her, but the ship was not up to such a journey. He could meet the commitments that had accumulated during his three-year journey from the publication of his account of the trip – *The North-West Passage* – and his earnings from numerous articles for *Harper's Monthly Magazine* in New York were not inconsiderable; but

Fridtjof Nansen, Norwegian Arctic explorer he made the first crossing of Greenland in 1888. Nansen got closer to the North Pole than anyone before him.

they were not sufficient for a new expedition. Even his lecture tour across Western Europe, with hand-coloured slides in his luggage, made him popular, but no richer. In London he addressed the Royal Geographical Society, in Paris the Societé de Géographie, in Berlin the Gesellschaft für Erdkunde before Kaiser Wilhelm II. Wherever he appeared, he was celebrated as the conqueror of the North-West Passage, but the tall, wiry Norwegian, dubbed the 'last Viking' by the European press, gained no friends. Recognition, yes, gold and silver medals, but not friends; his gaze was too cool and his manner too self-congratulatory. Amundsen discovered for the first time that popularity has a price – loneliness. He was still paying it without concern.

However, he had been able to buy himself a wooden house in 1908 – 'Uranienborg' on the Bundefjord. He decorated it with memories. He had transparencies of scenes of his North-West Passage journey applied to glass doors and individual ceiling lights. Everything and everyone was included, his Eskimo friends and the crew, friendship and happy days in the cold. 'Uranienborg' was a good house for a solitary man, large and strongly built; he had its rooms fitted out like ship's cabins. It was a land refuge, and he installed his former nanny, Betty, as housekeeper there; he could remain what he had always been at sea and in the ice – number one, implacable in desire, hysterical in frustration.

Houses reflect the personalities of their owners. Fridtjof Nansen's high, forbidding mansion 'Polhøgda' ('Polar Heights') was like a commanding castle atop a mountain amid thick forest. The view from its tower over the Christiania Fjord was overwhelming. 'Polhøgda' was like a metaphor in stone of its owner, aristocratic and with solid foundations in the Norwegian soil. Nansen, Nansen everywhere, the symbol of national confidence. Amundsen had only told one person of how he wanted to escape from Nansen's shadow and achieve what his role model had not; Leon, Amundsen's brother, had understood perfectly. Then, when they were on their winter tour through the mountains, Roald spoke of the North Pole. In 1906, on his return from his first great success, he thought of the Antarctic and the *Fram*; he wanted Nansen to give it to him so he could set off on his great venture. Should he say what he had in mind? Shackleton had headed for the very place he himself wanted to go, and Amundsen knew that Nansen was still toying with the thought of conquering the South Pole himself. The two men had spoken of it when Nansen was finding out about the *Belgica* expedition, and Amundsen listened carefully. The Antarctic, Nansen had said, thinking of himself, was flat, like the Greenland ice sheet, probably quite easy for good skiers to conquer, rather than being fragmented like the northern pack ice. Amundsen knew that his skills had now surpassed Nansen's both on skis and with dog sledges; but Nansen would not give him the *Fram*, at least not for a journey to the Antarctic, since he wanted to round off his own career with the conquest of the South Pole. But Amundsen, the younger man by 11 years, asked to be allowed to have the ship to repeat Nansen's drift and reach the North Pole. 'It may seem intrusive to you, but you will forgive the question, as you know how interested I am in the matter. Have you already made a decision about the journey which we discussed when I was in London in February? I would prefer to attach myself to you and could make myself useful; but if you cannot put your plans into effect, I would be very pleased to stick to my plan, or rather, your original plan, namely to travel through the Bering Strait before autumn and over the Pole.'

Because his political duty to Norway made any other decision impossible, Nansen gave the younger man the ship. 'If I had carried out my expedition first and left you the *Fram* afterwards, your own journey would have been put off too long, as I said to you at the time. And then, I thought in the end, your journey over the Polar Sea would be of greater scientific significance than my discovery of the South Pole and the measurements I would have been able to carry out there, and which someone else would be able to do just as well. With a heavy heart, I thus gave up the plan I had so long cherished and which would have crowned my life's work. I did this in favour of your journey; that seemed to me the better course and more useful for Norway. You were younger, with a great life's work still before you, whereas I could find other things to do. Yes, that's how it was; but it was only later that I realized how much it had cost me to abandon my long-cherished plans, though I hope I never let you see it.'

Nansen had decided against his dreams and, as Ibsen said, against the lie that he was capable of conquering the South

Pole for himself. Did Amundsen really intend to take the *Fram* through the northern pack ice and over the North Pole? On 10 November 1908 – the King of Norway was there, and many representatives of the diplomatic corps – Amundsen explained his plans.

'At the beginning of 1910 I would like to set off with the *Fram*, equipped for 7 years and with a good crew. I will set sail for San Francisco via Cape Horn, and take on coal and provisions there. Then to Port Barrow, the northernmost promontory of America, where we will send our last messages home before setting off on the journey itself. I intend to leave Point Barrow with the smallest possible crew. We will set a north-north-westerly course, and look for the most favourable point from which to get further north. Once we have found it, we will try and get as far as we can, and prepare ourselves for a journey of four or five years over the Polar Sea in the frozen ship … as soon as it has been frozen in, our research will begin; these should resolve some secrets which are so far unexplained.'

No-one asked why the *Fram* needed to sail round America to enter the icy northern sea. The route from Norway's northern cape east into the Bering Strait had often been taken, and was relatively well mapped. No-one asked why the conqueror of the North-West Passage wanted to avoid the North-East Passage. When Amundsen received the *Fram*, time was on his side. Shackleton was planning to have returned to England by 1910, and Scott could not start his expedition to the southern continent until then. Until Cape

Horn, the southernmost point of South America, he could decide where to steer the ship – further south, or half way round the world back to the north. He deceived them all, even Nansen, who wrote these passionate words about the meaning of polar exploration:

'It was the power of the unknown over the human spirit that drove men into the polar regions. As our conceptions have become clearer with the passage of time, this power has extended its rule and urged man willy-nilly further on the path of progress. It drives us to the hidden powers and secrets of nature, down into the immeasurably small microscopic world and also out into the unexplored regions of the universe ... It will leave us no peace until we know the planet on which we live from the uttermost depths of the ocean to the topmost layers of the atmosphere. This power runs like a red thread through the whole history of polar exploration. Despite everything that has been said about the potential usefulness of one area or another, it is this power that has always lead us back to it in the deepest recesses of ourselves, despite all setbacks and sufferings.'

Amundsen had thrown down a gauntlet on the Polar ice; no-one yet knew who was to pick it up, perhaps not even Amundsen himself. But when it came to it he would know, and still keep silent. Like a cardsharp, he would take a trump card out of his sleeve and take charge of the game.

Captain Scott and his wife Kathleen on the deck of the Terra Nova *after her arrival in New Zealand. It was to be their last farewell.*

5

Playing with Hidden Cards

*'As long as Englishmen do such things, we need not lie awake
at night worrying about an attack by the boys of the Dachshund
race.'*

Daily Telegraph, June 1909

*'With Shackleton, the English people have achieved a victory in
Antarctic exploration that can never be surpassed. What Nansen
is to the north, Shackleton is to the south.'*

Roald Amundsen

On 14 June 1909, Shackleton returned to London
from the Antarctic, not a moment too soon, for
the country needed men like him. He was given a
rousing welcome and knighted by the King. Amundsen sent
a telegram to the Royal Geographical Society from 'Uranienborg': 'I must congratulate you on the tremendous achievement. With Shackleton, the English people have achieved a
victory in Antarctic exploration that can never be surpassed.
What Nansen is to the north, Shackleton is to the south.'
So he had been right. Shackleton had had to give up his

advance towards the Pole about 175 kilometres before his goal. Shackleton later told his wife, 'I thought you would rather have a live donkey than a dead lion.'

Shackleton's expedition had done more than to reach the furthest point south. It was the first to reach the magnetic South Pole, and the first to ascend Mount Erebus, the volcano in the McMurdo Sound. Shackleton had proved that the South Pole lay on an ice cap similar to the Greenland Ice Sheet; he had also mapped out routes to the top, across a glacier, more than a hundred miles long, that he named the Beardmore in honour of his benefactor. Britain, though seriously threatened by the ambitions of imperial Germany and shaken by social unrest, had a new hero, sure of himself, lively and patriotic. 'I am representing 400 million British subjects,' Shackleton had said. The leader writers of the *Daily Telegraph* and the *Sphere* wrote, with an eye on Germany: 'In our age, filled with vain babbling about the decadence of the race, he has upheld the old fame of our breed. As long as Englishmen do such things, we need not lie awake at night worrying about an attack by the boys of the Dachsund race.' Shackleton might not have conquered the South Pole, but he had inspired the country, returning that oddly magical place to the public consciousness. Scott saw this as a challenge, and also his chance to get the necessary support for an attempt on the Pole. To be sure, Shackleton had begun his trek from the McMurdo Sound, breaking the agreement he had made, but Scott was clever enough not to make anything of this with him, especially as the Royal Geographical Society showed little inclination to intervene in the matter. 'Scott would make a very great mistake,' an official letter from the Society said, 'competing with Shackleton in organizing an expedition to go over the old route merely to do that 97 miles. The Council of the Royal Geographical Society is of the opinion that the Society ought not only to be neutral but actually opposed to it. Let Scott lead another Antarctic expedition if he will, but let it be a scientific expedition.'

Scott had to scheme, and seek out supporters. The smile on his face concealed his obsession with 'doing that 97 miles', just as it concealed his resentment about the man who had almost stolen the South Pole from him. He even acted as chairman at a dinner in honour of Shackleton in London's Savage Club, only to officially announce his own quest for the Pole amidst the applause of those present. 'All that remains now is for me to thank Mr. Shackleton for so nobly showing the way.' The two men were never to speak again; henceforward they avoided one another.

Like Scott, Amundsen too had trouble getting his Polar expedition off the ground. Once again, the problem lay in financing the project. The day after Amundsen had announced his journey to the North Pole in Christiania, the Norwegian King Haakon VII placed 30,000 kroner at his disposal; this soon meant that other donors wanted to become involved in the project. Amundsen's response to this enthusiastic stream of donations was on the terse side: 'The way people are showing their enthusiasm for the great national undertaking is truly moving.' But by the beginning of 1909, barely a quarter of the capital needed had been amassed, and the donations began to dry up. Amundsen summed up the situation as follows: 'People here think in a very mediocre and narrow-minded way, and it is necessary to work extraordinarily hard to drum up the funds required.'

The *Fram* was state-owned, and was in the naval dockyard at Horten on the Christiania Fjord. Though Nansen had given up his claim on the ship to Amundsen, permission to use the *Fram* still needed to be formally requested from the Storting, Norway's parliament. In January 1909 Amundsen submitted his request, also asking for 75,000 kroner to be granted for fitting-out the ship. The resulting debate in the Storting dragged on for some time, and meanwhile Nansen made a public appeal: Amundsen's expedition was of such great significance for Norway that no trouble should be spared in carrying it out. 'It is clear that it is especially important for a small nation to unite in the pursuit of cultural tasks when there is an opportunity, especially in fields where it is particularly talented. Here the little countries are in the same position as the big ones. By making great efforts in exploration, art or science, they lay claim to their status as independent nations and their significance in world culture. Every attempt of such a kind, large or small, is a contribution to increased confidence at home and recognition abroad.'

Amundsen himself went to London to explain on the spot the plans he had already sent to the Royal Geographical Society in writing. 'I should be most grateful to the Royal Geographical Society if it informed me of its views about my planned Arctic expedition. My application to the Norwegian parliament to be allowed to use the *Fram* will be debated early in January, and it would be most useful to have a response to hand before then.'

Sir Clements Markham congratulated Amundsen on this lecture, visibly relieved that he had set his sights on the northern hemisphere. 'I applaud the decision my friend Amundsen has taken to follow in the footsteps of Nansen. There is no getting around the fact that it will be a very dangerous undertaking. Like Nansen's undertaking, this is a splendid plan and one worthy of the man who first navigated the North-West Passage.' After this, Amundsen was received by Edward VII. 'It went very well, the King was very interested and asked lots of questions.' With the blessing of the English king, whose daughter Maud had been betrothed to Haakon VII since 1896, Amundsen returned to Christiania in good time for the debate in the Storting. The atmosphere in the Norwegian parliament was fairly heated, and the deputies argued vigorously. Amundsen's supporters put the patriotic case. 'Shall we really allow the Royal Geographical Society over there to say, good God, is the Norwegian nation too poor to provide 75,000 kroner for such a project?' The other side, the Social Democrats, were also worried about the international reputation of their country: 'If it became known in Europe that we have granted 75,000 kroner for Amundsen's project when it is also known that we let our schoolteachers go hungry, what would people think?' After a long debate over 70 per cent of the parliament voted in favour of

Amundsen's request; clearly, the blessing of England affected the outcome.

So the die was cast, and Norway had officially sanctioned Amundsen and the goal of his expedition, the North Pole. The *Fram* was taken out of the water, serviced, re-rigged as a schooner, and fitted with a new diesel engine. Amundsen was relieved, finding time alongside the intensive preparations for the expedition to begin an affair with Sigrid Castberg, wife of the lawyer Leif Castberg. There was talk of a divorce and of Sigrid marrying Amundsen.

Like Scott, Amundsen had great difficulty forming proper relationships with the opposite sex. Amundsen's character left room only for his passion for himself. He sought confirmation, unconditional respect, understanding and empathy, but without himself being able to give these things back to his partner. This pattern was firmly fixed, and events later repeated themselves, first in England, then later still in America. He always fell for married women whose husbands he knew; he always demanded an immediate and unconditional decision in favour of his feelings and his desires. If the woman he was pursuing hesitated, his enthusiasm quickly cooled, but he did not tell her. Amundsen feared scandal, and also the vengeance of rejected women. When one wife decided against her husband and in favour of a life with Amundsen, free at last after a long divorce, and was just about to board a ship bound from America to Norway, Amundsen cabled a brief apology; he was off once again to Polar regions, and so could not receive her. Sigrid Castberg, though, did not seriously consider separation from her husband, given the seven years Amundsen was due to spend frozen into the ice living far away from her. She had an affair with Amundsen that made them both happy for a month or two; she had a feeling for this man who experimented with using gliders to transport men and baggage, and had a collapsible wooden house built in the garden of 'Uranienborg'. She did not ask whether he intended to put up the house on the drifting ice of the Arctic; it was made by the same carpenter who had renovated 'Uranienborg' throughout, and he was very mysterious about it. No-one asked about it. Neither did she care about many other inconsistencies in his behaviour; all she cared about were the hours they spent in Christiania's Grand Hotel, which were kept a careful secret from the censorious inhabitants of the capital. In London, meanwhile, Scott was about to get married, before being officially named as the leader of a new Antarctic expedition.

Scott had met Kathleen Bruce, the daughter of a Scottish parson, in 1906. She had studied sculpture and worked as a nurse in the Balkan War, apart from having travelled widely elsewhere in Europe; she knew the dancer Isadora Duncan, the writer Gertrude Stein, and Picasso and Rodin. The two met at one of the London artists' parties at which Scott frequently made such a good impression, having been introduced to them by his sister Mabel. Kathleen Bruce later remembered this first meeting. 'He was standing over me. He was of medium height, with broad shoulders, very small waist, and dull hair beginning to thin, but with a rare smile, and with eyes of a quite unusually dark blue, almost purple. He suggested taking me home.'

To judge from his outward appearance, Scott could be taken for a ladies' man, but in fact he was anything but that, a rather shy man who preferred to admire strong, clever women from a distance. He still lived with his mother, who saw Kathleen for what she was, a rival. Mrs Scott strongly disapproved of the relationship; she hoped her son would marry rank and wealth. Scott wanted to free himself from his mother's influence by marrying Kathleen, finally becoming independent. He wrote love letters. 'Compared to yours, my personality is of no significance; it can neither inspire others nor satisfy them, but it succeeds by sheer persistence.' It soon seemed they would marry. 'I need someone to hang on to,' he wrote to his future wife, who admired him as a heroic Polar explorer. They were married on 2 September 1908 in the Chapel Royal at Hampton Court, setting off on a one-week honeymoon in France before moving into a flat not far from the Admiralty at 174 Buckingham Palace Road. Afterwards Scott resumed his service as captain of the battleship HMS *Bulwark*. 'You must go to the South Pole. My God, what use is all your energy and capability if you can't even manage that. It must be possible. So get on with it and leave no stone unturned.' Scott had married a woman with the ambition to help him overcome his own hesitatancy and his tendency to resign himself to the mounting disputes about his leadership abilities. A report on the scientific results of the *Discovery* expedition had come out, accusing Scott of serious errors, especially in carrying out the meteorological research programme. The press had a field day. 'The meteorological observations, instead of being made by people familiar with such work, were entrusted to officers who had no previous training, and were not even properly instructed. How much longer shall we have to wait in England for those entrusted with national affairs to appreciate a little more seriously the requirements of scientific investigation? Probably until the constant leakage and loss which we suffer in ignorance are made plainer by one or more exceptional disasters.'

At the end of the year Scott was appointed naval assistant to the Second Sea Lord, Admiral Sir Francis Bridgeman, which meant being recalled to London. He hesitated, but his wife made the decision for him: '... you don't see any grave reason against it. For working the Expedition it would be essential to be on the spot.' In addition, Kathleen Scott had managed to convince Sir Edgar Speyer, a City banker, to give her husband's expedition financial support, if it should come to pass. Scott accepted the appointment; apart from anything else, he had received a surprise telegram at the beginning of the next year. 'Throw up your cap & shout & sing triumphantly!' Kathleen Scott was pregnant. Now Scott began to undertake serious steps towards returning to the White Continent.

The *Discovery* had been sold to the Hudson Bay Company and was no longer available, so Scott set about obtaining the *Terra Nova* and an official commission from the Royal Geographical Society to take the ship with an expedition to the Ross Sea. He received their agreement surprisingly quickly; it was certainly influenced by the sensational news that the American Robert Edwin Peary had reached the North Pole on 6 September 1909. The South Pole became a matter of public interest. There was not much time left to be the first to reach it – after all, the Japanese and the Germans were preparing expeditions to the Antarctic too. On 13 September 1909 a British polar expedition, under the command of Captain Scott, was officially announced to the world in the *Times* and the *Daily Mail*; on the following day, Kathleen Scott gave birth to a son, who was baptized Peter Markham.

The news of the conquest of the northern Pole had also reached Norway, making people noticeably less inclined to invest money and equipment in Amundsen's Polar journey. Some firms went back on their promises of free supplies, donors demanded the return of loans and advances – even Lord Northcliffe, who had acquired the rights to report on the Polar expedition for £5,000. The race to the North Pole was over. Amundsen had a deficit of about 150,000 kroner. He asked the government for a further 25,000 kroner, but the Storting refused his request, which had once again emphasized the purely scientific character of the expedition. 'There are many people who believe that a Polar expedition is just a pointless waste of money and life. They generally associate the idea of a Polar expedition with the notion of a record, getting to the Pole or to a furthest north. I want to make it as clear as possible that such an assault on the Pole is not the aim of this expedition; its main aim is a scientific study of the polar sea itself, more precisely an investigation of the ocean floor and the oceanographic situation of this body of water.' He kept to himself the fact that he was more interested in the conquest of the Pole than the floor of the Arctic ocean. Once again he invested in the expedition money of his own that he did not really have, just as he had done when preparing for his journey through the North-West Passage. He took out a mortgage of 25,000 kroner on his house, and borrowed money recklessly wherever he could. If he returned to Norway as a hero, this mountain of debt could be dealt with. He entrusted the entire financial management of the expedition to his brother Leon so that he himself would be free to concentrate on the things that were really important to him. It must have been his brother whom he first let into the secret of the true goal of the expedition; the public still assumed it was going north.

In the autumn of 1909, during the flood of news about the conquest of the North Pole by Peary, a second American made his own claim to have got there first – it was Frederick Cook, who had travelled with Amundsen on the *Belgica*. When the latter was asked which of the two men he thought was lying, or whether both of them could actually have reached the Pole, Amundsen's answer to the *New York Times* was rather cool: 'It would be useless to make speculations as to the points arrived at by the two explorers. It is not important if the exact mathematical pole was reached or not, but it is important that the geographical conditions of the spot were observed. Probably something will be left to be done. What is left will be sufficient for all of us.'

What he did not say was that he was not going to be the man who would carry out further research into the geographical conditions; he returned to 'Uranienborg' to quietly prepare for the *Fram*'s voyage. 'I will permit myself to list here what I shall need: 50 dogs, 14 complete Eskimo outfits made of sealskin, 20 prepared sealskins for patching the suits with, 20 dog whips. As far as the dogs are concerned, it is essential that I have the best.' His initial order from the outfitter Daugaard-Jensen in Copenhagen was followed by a cable doubling the number of dogs required, and warning: 'If you get any other orders for dogs, I do hope you will remember that I got in first.' Amundsen was afraid that Scott would also buy dogs in Copenhagen, and as the Danish government had severely restricted the export of Greenland sledge dogs, he would then be forced to share the quota with his rival. This worry was unfounded; the British expedition stuck to their tradition that dogs, if needed at all, should come from Siberia. Daugaard-Jensen selected a hundred of the best Greenland dogs for Amundsen, but without asking why he was going to expose them twice over to the equatorial heat when he could have embarked huskies in Alaska.

Now that the North Pole had been conquered, Amundsen had finally made his decision; but he had to keep it to himself. Possibly Nansen would have insisted on his own claim on the voyage of discovery to the South Pole – at any rate, detailed plans for an Antarctic expedition were in his desk

– or Haakon VII's consort Maud would have told him Great Britain had a prior moral claim on the region, pointing out that Britain had always guaranteed Norwegian sovereignty. And was it not with help from London that he had managed to convince the Storting in the first place that Norway ought to undertake the journey into the northern pack ice as a national duty? If he were to reveal the true destination of the trip, that would be the end of it. Amundsen could not help thinking like this, so he kept everything to himself, and avoided any questions about the point of this or that decision during the preparations. Not even the crew could be told, at least at first; they were completely in his power. Each of them had signed the contract imposed by Amundsen. 'I undertake on my honour and conscience to obey the leader of the expedition or whichever person or persons he may designate as having authority in every way and for the entire duration of the trip, and also to obey all orders given to me immediately, and to undertake all tasks allotted to me.' He had to reveal his destination to one man, Lieutenant Thorvald Nilsen, his second-in-command, who had to know where they were going so he could make a thorough study of the appropriate charts. To avoid suspicion, Nilsen ordered the charts from London on some innocent pretext, using someone from the embassy as an intermediary. Even in London, nobody suspected a thing.

No-one apart from Amundsen's deputy and his brother had been let into the secret. The conqueror preferred to struggle on his own; when he had gained the victory, he would receive the laurels. Only this victory mattered – the South Pole. In comparison, everything else seemed unimportant. When Scott wrote to ask for a meeting to coordinate the scientific work of the two expeditions to the Antarctic and the Arctic, Amundsen excused himself by replying that he was too over-burdened by his preparations to make any commitments, let alone keep to them. Scott telephoned 'Uranienborg' several times from Christiania, where he was visiting Nansen with Kathleen, but Amundsen pretended to be out. The two men never met, but the thought of his English competitor would always be in Amundsen's mind.

The Scotts did not come to Christiania just to get Nansen's blessing for the British expedition, but also to try out a new development in the mountains to the west of the town, a chain-driven motorised sledge. In a paper, *The Sledging Problem in the Antarctic: Men versus Motors*, Scott had adopted an idea of the *Discovery* expedition's engineer, Reginald Skelton. 'I am of the opinion that a very high Southern Latitude could be achieved and the possibility of the South Pole itself could be reached by the proper employment of vehicles capable of mechanical propulsion over the surface of the Great Southern Barrier.' This was a brilliant idea, and Scott thought it would be the key to his success. 'I will only go South with a pretty good certainty of success and I believe that that can only be obtained by universal patience in getting the machine that is required.'

The trials near Christiania were promising, though not entirely satisfactory. But Scott could not and would not wait any longer, and thought that there was sufficient expertise aboard the *Terra Nova* to deal with any problems that might arise with the motors of the sledges. It was his intention to take three motorised sledges to the Antarctic, as well as Shetland ponies and Siberian dogs. In any case, Scott found it difficult to break the traditional mould, thinking that his men would be able to haul the sledges over snow and ice, as he had done himself. But Skelton, the engineer who had developed the sledges, was not to be included in the trip, and Scott would come to feel his absence sorely.

Scott was relying on the superiority of his equipment, whilst Amundsen counted on his experience with Greenland dogs and on the abilities of his men. Nansen recommended a young ski instructor to Scott, Tryggve Gran, who himself wanted to go on an Antarctic expedition and would be able to teach the British team how to use skis on the spot, if Scott would only take him with him. Scott wanted to cover all eventualities, so he signed Gran up so that he could teach his men how to ski at some point between the landing in the Antarctic and setting off for the Pole. The Ross Shelf, however, was no nursery slope.

On 6 May 1910, shortly before the *Terra Nova* was due to depart, Britain's flags flew at half mast. King Edward VII had died. Scott's biographers would later point out the parallels – when the *Discovery* set sail, England was burying Queen Victoria; now, it was King Edward. Ten days later Halley's Comet gave grounds for anxiety, causing many to fear the Day of Judgement was upon them. This was when

Gran arrived in London; the next day, he stood on the decks of the *Terra Nova*, which was still not ready to depart. On 31 May, the Royal Geographical Society gave a lunch in Scott's honour, and Major Leonard Darwin, Markham's replacement as president of the Society, toasted him: 'Scott is going to prove once again that the manhood of the nation is not dead and that the characteristics of our ancestors, who won this great empire still flourish amongst us.' Scott's answer was oddly frosty: 'We have the men necessary for the success of a polar expedition. But yet, complete as this provision seems to be, we cannot fail to realise that there are man other men in this great empire (and remember that I have tried to make this an empire expedition) who might greatly help forward our work.'

On 1 June 1910 the *Terra Nova* set off, its task having been blown up into a patriotic cause. One of the guests of honour, Captain Bartlett, an Anglo-Canadian with experience of the Polar regions, described his impression in the following comparison: 'Two things especially struck me, the attitude of the country and the kind of equipment; there were gold lace and cocked hats and dignitaries enough to run a Navy. I couldn't help comparing all this formality with the shoddy, almost sneering, attitude of the American public towards Peary's brave efforts. The basis of all Peary's work was the application of Eskimo methods. In contrast to this, the British worked out their own theories. They proved on paper that it wasn't worth while to use dogs. I thought of these things as I looked at the fine woollen clothing, the specially designed (in England) other gear. None of it looked like the Eskimo stuff that we were used to.'

Sir Clements Markham, honourable, white-haired, a fossil of a Victorian confidence that was already all but forgotten, had finally got his way after 30 years. The White Ensign was flew at the masthead of the *Terra Nova*. The fact that the British Antarctic Expedition sailed under this flag was an expression of the navy's claim to rule the world's oceans – probably a deliberate demonstration of its power at a time when Europe was heading for war.

They set off down the Thames, and then a cruiser towed the ship to Portland. The young Gran was duly impressed by this show of naval strength: 'At that time, the British Home Fleet – the world's mightiest naval force – lay gathered in Portland Harbour. Little *Terra Nova* – decorated with flags from topmast to deck, steamed as it were through a crowded street of battleships and battlecruisers. On the decks of the armoured colossi, the crews were drawn up alongside the railings, and the cheers from the many thousands of throats fairly made the air quiver on that blazing summer afternoon.' After taking on coal in Cardiff, the *Terra Nova* left the British coast behind. Gran wrote in his diary: 'Neither before or since in time of peace have I heard such an uproar as that which made the air tremble as *Terra Nova* glided out through the docks. People in their thousands yelled as if they had taken leave of their senses. Railway wagons were rolled over a line covered with dynamite detonators, and vessels in their hundreds completed the noise with whistles and sirens.

At the last lock gates we were met by a little squadron of beflagged boats, and with this as escort we steamed out into the open sea.'

It was 15 June 1910; the *Fram* had already been at sea for a week.

Since 3 June, *Fram* had lain off Amundsen's house on the Bundefjord, outside Christiania. The crew took the wooden hut apart, carefully numbering the individual parts ready for reconstruction before loading it on board. On the night of 7 June, the anniversary of Norwegian independence, Amundsen ordered the anchor to be raised. *Fram* glided slowly out into the fjord. 'Set off at midnight,' began Amundsen's first entry in his diary of the voyage. 'We are departing from the Christiania fjord in quiet and calm mood. Soon we will be out of sight of land, and *Fram* will have begun her journey. God grant that we acquit ourselves well!'

Fridtjof Nansen, in the tower of 'Polhøgda' on the other side of the fjord, was among those watching the departure of the *Fram*. Years later he admitted that it was the bitterest moment of his life. His wife had died aboard the ship that he regarded as the symbol of his own life had had to be passed on to a younger man. Nansen must have felt lost. He did not yet know that that man had betrayed him.

Amundsen had deceived them all, two royal families, the European geographical societies, the public. He had led both Nansen and Scott up the garden path. What is more, he concealed the true goal of their journey from the crew, at least until Madeira. He did not know, though, that he had deceived himself; he never would, though he may often have had an inking of it. In Funchal, the port of Madeira, he had to put his cards on the table. He waited till the last moment so he could make a dramatic impression. The anchor chain had already been half hauled in when he called the crew on deck. While Leon Amundsen, who had been sent out ahead on a liner to the island of Madeira to get fresh fruit, water and two horses slaughtered for the dogs ready to be loaded conveniently, came out to the ship in a rowing boat, Nilsen, the first mate, nailed a map of the Antarctic onto the mainmast. Then Amundsen stood in front of his men and explained as if in passing that he planned to make a detour to the South Pole *en route* to the North Pole. 'There are many things on board that you have regarded with suspicion or surprise, the observation hut or the dogs; but that is not what I want to speak about now. What I want to say is that it is my intention to travel southward and set down a landing party on the southern continent to try and reach the South Pole.'

Of course, he continued, he would stick to their destination, but the North Pole would have to wait a while; the important thing now was to beat the British. Anyone who wanted to leave the crew was free to go, and would receive his pay. None of the men was able or willing to turn away from the influence of their leader, all were subject to his will. Helmer Hanssen, who had already shown his reliability as helmsman and guide through the ice on board the *Gjøa*, later wrote in his diary: 'When we came to reflect on it, everyone said, why did you say yes like that? If you had said no, I would have too.'

Then Leon Amundsen left the ship with hastily-written letters to relatives at home, and three letters from his brother, one to the King of Norway, one to the press, and one to Nansen.

'Professor Fridtjof Nansen, it is with an uneasy heart that I write these lines to you; but because there is no getting round it, the best thing will be for me to come straight to the point. Only one unsolved problem in the Polar regions remained through which the interest of the masses could be gained, the conquest of the South Pole. Indeed, it is not easy for me to admit to you, Professor, that as early as September 1909 I had already made the decision to take part in the contest for the solution of this matter. At times I was on the point of telling you all, but each time I decided not to, fearing that you might hinder me. So since September of last year my decision has been made, and I may say well prepared for.

We shall sail south from Madeira to South Victoria Land. There I intend to land with 9 men and send the *Fram* on an oceanographic cruise. I have not yet decided where we will land, but I do not intend to follow the English. They have the first claim and we must make do with what they do not want. *Fram* will return in February or March 1912 to take us off. Then we will sail to Lyttelton in New Zealand in order to send a cable there, before continuing to San Francisco so that I can resume my interrupted task with, as I hope, the equipment needed for such a journey.

When you pass judgement on me, Professor, do not be too severe. I have taken the only path that seemed open to me, and now things must take their course.

The King will be informed at the same time as you receive this letter, but no-one else. A few days later, my brother will announce the changes to the plan of my expedition. Once again I ask you not to treat me too severely. I am not a trickster, but did what I had to do. I ask your pardon for what I have done. May the work that lies ahead be a penance for my failings. Yours with the greatest respect, Roald Amundsen.'

*One of Captain Scott's encampments made on the crossing of the
Beardmore Glacier, 1911.*

6

Meeting on the
Edge of the Ice Shelf

*'I was waked at one o'clock by Lillie with the astounding news
that we had sighted a ship at anchor to the sea ice in the Bay.
All was confusion on board for a few minutes, everybody rushing
up on deck with cameras and clothes. There she was within a few
hundred yards of us and what is more, those of us who had read
Nansen's books recognized the* Fram.'

Raymond Priestley

*'We spent a few jolly hours together, and later in the day, three of
us paid a visit on board the* Terra Nova *and stayed for brunch.'*

Roald Amundsen

I t was seven years since Scott had left Hut Point, the
expedition's winter quarters deep in the McMurdo
Sound, in the *Discovery*; at the beginning of January
1911, he saw Mount Erebus and its plume of smoke once
again. But he was not able to get very far, because *Terra
Nova*'s route to the old winter base was blocked by pack ice.
He was forced to pick a landing place below the volcano's

foothills, on a promontory made up of rocks and moraine. He named this place, a promontory of Ross Island, Cape Evans, 'in honour of our excellent second in command', who had saved the ship from foundering in the storm. It was 4 January. '4 pm. About 2 miles from the shore the ship ran into solid ice, offering a route to the Cape and a tenable surface for disembarking our supplies. We secured ourselves to it with ice anchors and Wilson, Evans and I walked to the Cape. A glance at the land round about revealed the ideal spot for our winter station. A beach facing north-west, protected from behind by numerous hills, appeared to combine all the advantages of a winter station, and so we selected this spot on which to erect our house. After a lot of scolding Lady Luck has cheered us with a friendly smile!' Scott ordered the ship to be unloaded; but Lady Luck's smile would prove to have been deceptive.

The crew's direct route south from Cape Evans, past crevasses, cracks and ice falls up the ice barrier, was blocked; only experienced mountaineers could have got through. Realizing this, Scott relied on the sea ice, which stretched further southwards in the McMurdo Sound, as the only possible path. He also knew that the ice would become progressively weaker as the season advanced, so that he did not have much time left to transport all the material needed for a decisive assault on the Pole from Cape Evans over the ice shelf – ponies and dogs, food and fuel, sledges, tents and skis. He did not know how little time he really had. Just short of three weeks later, the situation had changed markedly. Early in the morning of 23 January, they saw that the ice had broken up into icebergs overnight, which were slowly drifting out to sea. Apart from an extremely narrow strip of ice, Cape Evans was cut off from the planned southward route. 'Once I had taken the situation in, we went at it hammer and tongs. All the sledges, all our equipment, even the dogs and the pony tackle, were brought aboard, and only the ponies are to make another attempt tomorrow to reach the tip of the glacier along the southward route. There they will be loaded again and we will begin our depot journey with the march to Hut Point. We cannot risk the lengthy uncertainty and possible delay of waiting for all the ice to drift out and let the ship get to Hut Point. I pray to God that the pony's route holds for the few remaining hours!'

Fortunately, it proved possible to drive the ponies along the narrow ice bridge from Cape Evans to Hut Point, the former winter quarters of the *Discovery*. All their remaining supplies, everything that was needed for the march to the South Pole, was loaded back onto the ship, having been unloaded three weeks before with considerable effort. The men worked all day and all night. Six miles up the sound, everything was unloaded again, which also took time. Only then did Scott send off his ship, with instructions to land two geological exploration teams at different points. Thursday 'January 26. The last day aboard the *Terra Nova*. Captain Pennell turned out the crew on the aft deck and I thanked them all for their hard work. They have all behaved like brave chaps, and a more splendid company has never sailed on a

Amundsen and Oscar Wisting with a few of the forty-six dogs that accompanied the expedition to the South Pole. They were the mainstay of its success.

ship. Their hearty cheers truly did me good.' The *Terra Nova* sailed to the western shore of the McMurdo Sound to put the first group of scientists ashore on Victoria Land, and then further east at a respectable distance along the Ross Barrier to King Edward VII Land, at the other end of the ice shelf.

Meanwhile, *Fram* too was offloading its cargo in the Bay of Whales. Roald Amundsen's diary entry on the first day's work in the Antarctic begins with the same high emotion with which Scott's entry ended. '15 January 1911. There it lies, the Barrier, just as it probably has done for thousands of years, bathing in the rays of the midnight sun. It looks as if the Princess is still sleeping in her crystal castle. If only we could wake her!' The first sledge was hoisted over the railing onto the ice and loaded with 300 kilograms of supplies; eight dogs were harnessed to it. Amundsen was to be the first to traverse the four kilometres, marked out with blue flags, up onto the shelf ice, but the honour of this first journey turned into a farce, to the amusement of all. 'The dogs, after they had gone a few paces, sat down as if on command, and stared at one another. With a crack of the whip, we gave them to understand that we expected them to work, but that didn't help much either. Instead of obeying, they turned on each other in a glorious battle – goodness, we had a lot of trouble with those eight dogs on that day. In the midst of all the fuss, I glanced quickly back at the ship, but it was better to look away again. Everyone was bent over double with laughter as they shouted scurrilous suggestions at us.' The dogs did not take to the Canadian system of harnessing them. It was during his journey through the North-West Passage on the *Gjøa* that Amundsen had learned the method used in Alaska, where the dogs were harnessed in pairs to a single trace. Now he had to reconsider. His dogs came from Greenland and were used to running separately, in a fan-shaped array of harnesses. Using the whip was no more help than cajoling them, and the other dogs also refused to pull the sledge. The men had to rework the harnesses, but the results were well worth the effort. The huskies allowed themselves to be hitched up and raced up the icy incline, to the spot where the expedition would set up its base camp. The drivers kept up on skis if they were going uphill with a full load, but on the way down they rode on the empty sledges. The men worked 12-hour days, but the dogs only in five-hour shifts, as they did not want to wear them out. An average of ten tons of equipment was taken up onto the ice shelf each day, sometimes more, and while team after team deposited their burdens onto the loose snow on top of the ice shelf, the *Fram*'s two carpenters reassembled the hut from the Bundefjord. Stubberud would always remember the unusual working conditions for their task, 'the permanent drift of snow, filling up the workshop quicker than we could shovel it away'. While he and Bjaaland kept busy putting up their accommodation, others went hunting to lay in enough stores for a year. The game was prepared, and then kept safe from the ever-hungry huskies in a specially dug-out ice cellar. Two hundred seals were killed, as well as many penguins. 'It's like the land of milk and honey, the seals come up to the ship, penguins right up to the tent, and let us shoot them.' When some of the men went on a killing spree, leaving the carcasses behind on the ice, Amundsen's reaction was clear – not because of fondness for animals, but because he knew that an enthusiasm for hunting could undermine his authority. 'The members of the expedition are strictly forbidden to kill animals for which we have no use.'

By the end of January, the hut on the shelf ice where the Polar team would winter was finished. The base camp was ready for use, the starting-point on their path to success. Amundsen wrote: 'We have put up our house here, on the same ice barrier where Shackleton thanked God that he had not landed; this will be our home. There is no-one among us who feels that there is anything dangerous in it. Time will tell if we are right.'

The landing party left the ship and made themselves at home in Framheim, as the men christened their winter quarters. There continued to be plenty of work, and everyone knew what to do. Three advance depots with supplies for the polar journey had to be set up, there were various pieces of equipment which needed altering to suit the Antarctic climate, and the sledges needed to be converted. Amundsen brilliantly planned every detail of his attack on the Pole, leaving nothing to chance. Furthermore, he made sure his men had plenty to do so they did not have too much time to think. Would the shelf ice hold, or would it break off to form a giant ice floe, carrying Framheim out into the open sea? And when would the *Terra Nova* appear in the Bay of Whales with the British expedition?

On 4 February, shortly before midnight, they found out, still tied up on the edge of the ice barrier. Gjertsen, *Fram*'s second mate, rushed up on deck because he heard an odd noise that sounded like ice breaking up. It was in fact the *Terra Nova*'s ice anchors being thrown down to secure the ship. 'We had long since been expecting them to arrive in

the bay, as they were under way with a group going east to
King Edward VII Land. I saw two men go ashore, put on
skis and race up the ice barrier with extraordinary speed,
for foreigners. If they should have ill intentions (one of our
constant topics of conversation was how the British would
respond to our challenge), the dogs would be able to deal
with it and make them turn round. But it would be more
worrying if they came and nosed around on the *Fram* during
my watch.' The two Englishman had seen enough of the
Ross Barrier, and turned round to make for *Fram*. Gjertsen
waited for them, a loaded weapon and an English dictionary
in his hands.

The *Terra Nova* had left McMurdo Sound on 28 January
to put down a landing party on King Edward VII Land
under the command of Lieutenant Victor Campbell. This
party of geologists was supposed to investigate the previously unexplored area at the eastern end of the Ross Barrier.
But their landing was hindered by thick pack ice and capri-
cious currents, and the ship retreated westwards in search
of a quiet anchorage. It was almost ten o'clock when the
Terra Nova steamed into the Bay of Whales; from here the
geologist Raymond Priestley, who had already been here with
Shackleton, was hoping to be able to reach King Edward VII
Land. 'It was satisfactory to find everyone backing up the
Shackleton expedition and I felt quite cheerful, believing
that there would be a good chance of finding a home on
the Barrier here – our last hope of surveying King Edward's
Land. However, man proposes but God disposes and I was

waked at one o'clock by Lillie with the astounding news that we had sighted a ship at anchor to the sea ice in the Bay. All was confusion on board for a few minutes, everybody rushing up on deck with cameras and clothes. There she was within a few hundred yards of us and what is more, those of us who had read Nansen's books recognized the *Fram*.'

The crew had expected Amundsen to be almost anywhere else, in the Weddell Sea or on Graham Land, whose coast must be very familiar to him as the former helmsman on board the *Belgica*, but certainly not here in the Ross Sea, the region the British claimed for themselves. So the excitement aboard *Terra Nova* was considerable. Scott's brother-in-law Wilfred Bruce later told Kathleen Scott that 'an eruption of Erebus would fall flat after that. Curses loud and deep were heard everywhere.' Campbell and his first officer, Lieutenant Pennell – who was to return the *Terra Nova* to New Zealand as Captain before the Antarctic winter set in – set off to scout out the terrain, as it were. Finding nothing on the edge of the ice shelf but an endless white desert, the appeared relieved, and set off on a direct approach to the Norwegian ship. Campbell wanted to take the bull by the horns, and surprised Gjertsen by addressing him in Norwegian, having mastered the language of Norway's mountains as well as how to ski when he was there. Gjertsen was nonplussed and was only able to tell the commander of the *Terra Nova* that Amundsen and his men were up on the ice barrier in their hut, and were expected to return early in the morning.

Amundsen had observed the arrival of the *Terra Nova* from

Framheim, and hoped that the Englishmen would withdraw once they had satisfied their curiosity. He had no particular desire for a meeting. They would ask him to explain why he had insinuated secretly himself into the British region, or else why he had pretended to be out when Scott had kept trying to contact him in Christiania. He had no time for debates about moral values or the code of honour of British polar explorers. He wanted to create facts, appearing before the world as a great victor with the Pole in his pocket. Then no-one would bother to ask how the conquest was achieved – just as long as it happened.

The visitors stayed, and Amundsen knew that his trump card had been revealed. Scott now knew his opponent's position. So Amundsen might as well go over to the *Terra Nova* to try and find out about the use of the three motorised sledges; he feared their power and speed. Towards six o'clock he went across to the ship with his men, having hitched up the finest of his dogs.

This spectacle had the intended effect. Gjertsen described the scene in his diary. 'They really raced down to the ship. The Englishmen were totally surprised. They had never expected dogs to be able to run like that before a sledge, and immediately started to have doubts abut their good old ponies. Suddenly they were gripped by excitement, cheering and waving their caps. Our drivers returned their greeting and cracked their whips.'

Amundsen invited the officers and men of the *Terra Nova* aboard the *Fram* to show them his famous ship. Once again, the newcomers were impressed. 'They all praised our comfortable and attractive quarters, and when they saw that each crewman had his own cabin as well as the large saloon, their eyes grew wide with astonishment.' Conditions on the British ship were rather different. 'Their mess table,' a sailor told Gjertsen and others, 'was right under the ponies, who produced "yellow mustard" to go with their meals.' 'Using the sanitary facilities,' he continued, 'was a question of balancing over a chute on the side of the ship above the ocean deeps. One of the crew of the *Fram* felt so sorry for them that he gave the downhearted sailor a glass of aquavit to cheer him up.' The officers were impressed too, though they kept it to themselves. 'The ship is wonderfully constructed and the officers' quarters are princely.' The Norwegian reaction on their return visit to the *Terra Nova* was unanimous. 'It really doesn't look that appealing.' But this meeting on the edge of the ice shelf went off peacefully, and the two parties vied in offering one another friendly encouragement. The Norwegians thought Scott's crew were 'good-natured and very friendly', and Wilfred Bruce found the *Fram*'s crew 'all seemed charming men, even the perfidious Amundsen'.

Campbell, Pennell and the doctor of the King Edward VII Land expedition were invited to brunch by Amundsen up on the ice at Framheim. The food seemed modest to the English party, despite the efforts of Adolf Henrik Lindstrøm, once cook aboard the *Gjøa*, to entertain his guests. The conversation at table was stilted, but this was because of Framheim itself rather than deficiencies in Lindstrøm's talents as a chef. Fourteen 16-man tents had been put up around the hut, some for storage, others to accommodate the dogs. Amundsen believed that huskies would best maintain condition when not working if they were protected against the cold and blizzards. Like most of the British expedition, Campbell had not believed that dogs might be well-suited to being draught animals in the Polar regions, but now he saw he had been wrong, and also how determined Amundsen was to beat Scott to the Pole. He must have been impressed with how efficiently Amundsen had prepared his expedition. Everything was subordinate to the single goal of beating Scott, whereas the conquest of the Pole was not even the official aim of the British expedition, which was a scientific voyage made up of several parties, of which one was to explore King Edward VII Land, and another group Victoria Land and the Ross Barrier; the Norwegian undertaking was a campaign of conquest. Lieutenant Campbell had enough strategic sense to see which side had the upper hand. He must also have been disappointed that the presence of the Norwegians had scuppered the idea that they could still reach King Edward VII Land overland, setting off over the shelf ice from the Bay of Whales. He himself would have been glad to take Amundsen up on his suggestion of setting up a British base next door to Framheim, but the others were against it. 'We cannot according to etiquette trench on their country for winter quarters,' Priestley said, expressing the feeling of the entire British party. In any case, Amundsen was convinced that Campbell would reject his offer, as he would otherwise be exposed to the wrath of the entire British nation at the intrusion of the Norwegians in a region traditionally declared to be part of the British domain. Amundsen could afford to be generous. Whatever the crew of the *Terra Nova* decided, he would be the moral victor in any case. Still, he was relieved not to have them at his back door; their presence close at hand would have disrupted his timetable considerably. Campbell must have seen through Amundsen's game; perhaps that is why he switched from Norwegian to English, a language Amundsen understood only with difficulty. They moved from talking shop to polite conversation.

That day, 4 February, was the one and only opportunity there would be to end the energetically-pursued competition for the Pole before it really got under way. But Lieutenant Campbell was not man enough to carry the day against those like Bruce whose false conception of honour made them convinced that 'the feeling between the two expeditions must be strained'. If the British landing party that was to explore King Edward VII Land had been put down next door to Framheim, Amundsen's preparations would have been delayed, but the arrival of Scott on the scene would have been quite possible. It is conceivable that their rivalry might have developed into some sort of collaboration. Certainly, Scott would then have been spared the profound psychological blow of being only the second man to reach the South Pole. But this opportunity was all too carelessly thrown away in favour of patriotic thinking and also the burden of expectation that lay on Scott; what might have been a historic moment became the occasion for idle chatter and considerations of etiquette. Amundsen, Nilsen and Kristian Prestrud were invited to lunch on the *Terra Nova*.

Amundsen was known to be a law unto himself, and he was visibly relieved when he saw that the British did not have a radio on board. He wanted to announce the victory, or defeat, of his expedition to the world himself, but not to provide a running commentary, still less to be the subject of gossip in English-language newspapers. The meal was excellent, and the drinks too suited the visitors well; the atmosphere appeared relaxed, but both sides knew what to expect. Casually, Amundsen asked about the motorised sledges. 'One of them,' Campbell replied, 'is already on terra firma.' This worried Amundsen; if one sledge was already on dry land, that must mean that it had been used successfully on the ice, and had perhaps already reached the Beardmore Glacier.

What Campbell did not say was that 'terra firma' meant the sea bed. When Scott's men unloaded the first sledge at Cape Evans in the middle of January, intending to pull it onto safe ground, the ice broke under its weight. Many hands held fast to the rope to save the sledge from sinking, but its weight made the rope cut through the ice faster and faster, and the men feared it might drag them into the water too so let it go. Since then, it had rested on the bottom of the McMurdo Sound, on 'terra firma'. The conversation dried up. Amundsen refused to talk about his own plans, pointing out that Campbell had refused his offer of collaboration, and the lunch on board the *Terra Nova* was soon at an end. Politely, but coolly, the men took their leave, but not without wishing one another luck. Half an hour later the *Terra Nova* sailed away, ten hours after they had arrived in the Bay of Whales. The die was cast.

As the British ship disappeared in the distance, Amundsen appeared nervous. He had thought everything through, calculated every possibility, but perhaps he had underestimated the capabilities of the motorised sledges. Though he did not seriously believe that technology posed a threat to his dog teams, he could not be quite sure. On 10 February, he set off to scout out the route southwards and find a suitable spot for the first depot. He was happy to be heading south at last. 'The skiing conditions could not have been better.' Beforehand, he took his leave of the ship's crew, that would take *Fram* from the pack ice, which would soon become thicker. He left written orders for Nilsen. 'According to the plan we worked out together,' Nilsen was to sail to Buenos Aires before conducting an oceanographic cruise and returning at the end of winter to relieve Framheim. 'The sooner you manage to get back to the Bay of Whales in 1912 the better. I am setting no fixed time, because everything will depend on the circumstances, and I leave it up to you to act according to your own judgement. In other respects, you have complete freedom in everything relating to the interests of the expedition. If it transpires when you return that because of sickness or death I am not able to lead the expedition, I place it in your hands, and urge you to carry out the original plan of the expedition, the exploration of the North Polar Basin. With gratitude for the time that we have spent together, and hoping that when we see each other next each of us will have attained his goal, your devoted Roald Amundsen.'

Meanwhile, the *Terra Nova* was back in McMurdo Sound, and Scott was told about the meeting with the Norwegian party. 'Our thoughts are full, too full of them. The impression they have left with us is that of a set of men with distinctive personalities, hard and evidently inured to hardship, good goers and pleasant good humoured men. We have news which will make Scott as uneasy as ourselves,' wrote Priestley in his diary. So that Scott could get sight of Campbell's report as soon as possible, Pennell took the ship up the sound to the old *Discovery* hut, hoping to find the leader of the expedition there. But Scott was on a depot journey, and would not receive Campbell's written report until two weeks later. The *Terra Nova* turned around and set course for the tip of South Victoria Land to land Campbell's exploration party on Cape Adare, close to Borchgrevink's old camp. While Campbell and his men prepared for the coming Antarctic winter, Pennell set sail for New Zealand, where he would tell the world of the meeting of *Fram* and *Terra Nova* in the Bay of Whales.

On 23 February, Scott read Campbell's report. Cherry-Garrard, who had been taken as a private member of the expedition in return for a payment of £1,000, was Scott's tent mate on the depot journey. 'For many hours, Scott could think of nothing else nor talk of anything else. Evidently a great shock for him – he thinks it very unsporting since our plans for landing a party there were known.' His reaction was tempestuous, and he lost his smile and his self-control. He shouted; later on, summarizing the day's events in his sleeping bag, he had pulled himself together again. 'Amundsen's proceedings have been very deliberate, and success alone can justify them. That the action is outside one's own code of honour is not necessarily to condemn it and under no condition will I be betrayed into a public expression of opinion. One thing only fixes itself definitely in my mind: to go forward and do our best for the country without fear or panic.' During the night he realized that Amundsen had it in him to beat them all, Shackleton, Scott himself and all previous British expeditions. 'There is no doubt that Amundsen's plan is a very serious menace to ours. He has a shorter distance to the Pole by 60 miles – I never thought he could have got so many dogs safely to the ice. His plan for running them seems excellent. But above and beyond all he can start his journey early in the season – an impossible condition with ponies.' Scott did not sleep well, but he did not come up with any practical plans to stave off the perhaps already inevitable defeat. 'The next morning, according to Cherry-Garrard, Scott jumped out of his bag & said, "By Jove, what a chance we have missed – we might have taken Amundsen & sent him back in his ship."' Many agreed with this, and some were still ready to do it. Even Tryggve Gran, Scott's Norwegian ski instructor, was shaken. 'It felt as though the Barrier had opened up beneath me, and my head was full of a thousand thoughts. Should I compete against my compatriots and my own flag?' Everyone looked to Scott, without quite knowing what to expect of him in such a situation. Captain Oates, who was also making the trip as a paying guest just for love of adventure and was responsible for the ponies, observed: 'If it comes to a race, Amundsen will have a great chance of getting there as he is a man at this kind of game all his life and he has a hard crowd behind him while we are very young.'

Scott concealed his uncertainty behind a nervous busyness, giving orders and then immediately contradicting them, showing himself everywhere but with his mind elsewhere. Eventually, he called everyone together and announced his decision: 'to go forward and do our best for the country without fear or panic!' This was not what the men were expecting, but they were glad to have someone to tell them what to do. Scott spoke as though trying to convince himself. The expedition, he said, had been sent to explore the unknown continent scientifically, not to participate in a race for the Pole. Neither the Crown nor Scott himself wanted to see such a contest. Amundsen's presence on the Ross ice did nothing to change this, he continued, and all the research projects would be carried out as planned without any pressure. In any case, Amundsen did not have the Pole in the bag, and he still had half a continent ahead of him. 'We must go forward and do our best for the country without fear or panic! God save the King and the British science explorer!' The cheering of the men lacked enthusiasm, but Scott took it as a confirmation of his intention to stop worrying about Amundsen and to wipe out the Norwegian incursion into the region he claimed for himself. What he kept to himself was that he still believed he would beat Amundsen to the South Pole. Scott remained convinced that dog teams were incapable of covering such a distance

Since 31 March 1911, when Pennell had arrived back in New Zealand aboard the *Terra Nova*, the whole world had known of Amundsen's secret base camp on the Ross Barrier, and the contest for the South Pole was the subject of intense interest. The British press even described Amundsen's coup as muscling in on the British exploration. In Norway, too, the mood changed. Benjamin Vogt, the Norwegian ambassador in London, observed anxiously: 'Very many people here think the way Amundsen has behaved is not fair or gentlemanly. Because of the state of public opinion, I am not exactly looking forward to hearing that A. has reached the South Pole first.' Sir Clements Markham spoke of Amundsen's 'dirty trick', calling him both a blackguard and an interloper; Shackleton's contemptuous conclusion was that Amundsen was 'wintering in Scott's sphere of influence'. Fridtjof Nansen, whose views carried weight in England, published a plea for his countryman in the *Times*. But this did nothing to alter the implicit condemnation of Amundsen's Antarctic journey in his own country.

When Nilsen anchored in the River Plate on 17 April, he was the first to be affected by this change of mood. The *Fram* needed to be overhauled, and the crew were expecting their pay; Amundsen had doubled it when he had told the crew of his new plans in Funchal. However, there were no funds in the expedition's account in Buenos Aires, since the Norwegian government had not dared to ask the Storting to advance any more money; after all, it had approved the financing of an expedition to the Arctic, not to the Antarctic. Nilsen's only recourse, against his inclinations, was to hold out his cap. He approached a Norwegian who had emigrated to Argentina in 1871, where he made his fortune in property. Peter Christophersen, universally known as Don Pedro, had offered a year before to pay for the diesel for the ship's engine should the *Fram* call at Buenos Aires *en route* to the Arctic. Leon Amundsen also sent a telegram to Argentina from Christiania asking for support: 'When my brother received your generous offer before his departure from Norway, he had no idea that he would need to take it up to the degree that now seems necessary; he was convinced that his sponsors and the Norwegian people would support his decision to go southwards, because his reasons for doing so where so compelling ... he firmly believed he could count on the necessary support for the journey. He still believes that he can. He is not yet aware that his behaviour has been so widely condemned, and when he finds out his sense of honour will be deeply wounded, and he will be overcome with great bitterness.' Both the expedition's financial troubles and its current negative image were well known to Don Pedro, yet he kept his word, paying for *Fram*'s refit, which after 20,000 miles at sea was essential. This generous gesture made Nilsen feel rather ashamed. He wrote to Leon Amundsen, the Antarctic expedition's business manager: 'It is unfair to ask so much of one individual. It is easy enough for people back home to say that the expedition went south in secret, so it ought to solve its own problems.'

Nilsen's disappointment at the reaction of the Norwegian government, which as he rightly suspected was intended to appease the British, was tempered by a letter he then received from Nansen, who was delighted at *Fram*'s coming oceano-graphic crossing from South America to South Africa. 'This part of the ocean has remained to some extent an unknown world in which previous expeditions have achieved little, or nothing significant. It would be splendid if Norwegians could show their superiority in this area too. This also clearly shows that the *Fram*'s expedition is more than a sporting feat; it is a scientific project that deserves to be respected.' On 8 June, the *Fram* headed off into the Atlantic. Meanwhile, the storms of winter raged on the Antarctic continent.

c

Captain L E G Oates stands on deck with four of the eight ponies taken on the expedition. The animals were so ill-suited to polar conditions that they would all perish.

7

Initial Preparations on the Ross Ice Shelf

'Any attempt to enter the race would have disrupted my plans. In any case, we did not set out on a race.'

Captain Scott

'There are many men who believe that polar expeditions are just a pointless waste of money and lives. They usually think of a polar expedition as being about a polar record ... I wish to make it crystal clear that this race to the Pole will not be the aim of the expedition.'

Roald Amundsen

The outcome of the race to the Pole was decided in men's heads, as the solution to a logistical problem.

After Cape Evans, there would be about 3,000 kilometres to cover, 1,500 there and 1,500 back. But the Norwegian base camp, Framheim, was about 150 kilometres closer to this goal, meaning that Amundsen's journey was shorter by double that distance, 300 kilometres. This was a decisive advantage, but one that could easily be thrown away if he did not take full advantage of it. Amundsen had already outlined his plans to do so at the Bundefjord, and now he set about putting them into action. He intended to spend 100 days on the journey with his Polar team, perhaps a few days more, advancing an average of 28 kilometres per day – assuming the weather and the dogs cooperated. How much food would eight men need on the way to the Pole, and how much would the dogs need? How much pemmican, a food concentrate consisting of a mixture of dried meat and melted fat that was traditionally used on Polar journeys? How much paraffin would be needed to cook the food? He had planned everything down to the smallest detail, without neglecting to include adequate safety margins. Because he did not entirely trust the commercial brands of pemmican, he had had the quantity he needed prepared according to his own recipe in an old bakery under the supervision of a chemist. On his own journey through the North-West Passage he had discovered how quickly liquid paraffin can evaporate from even carefully-sealed canisters, so he had them welded shut. Scott would complain constantly about the insufficient quantities of fuel in his depots, as his paraffin drums were almost half-empty when he opened them; they had been sealed in the traditional way with leather strips. In any case, he did not depot sufficient amounts in the first place.

On 10 February 1911, while the *Fram* was still at anchor at the edge of the ice shelf, Amundsen set off with three men, three sledges and 18 dogs to set up his first depot, at 80 degrees South. The young Prestrud went ahead on skis, with the three sledges behind him in a line; the huskies needed a leader to follow, and Prestrud was good at finding the way in the white desert. He went due south, with only the occasional minor correction from Helmer Hanssen, who was carrying the first compass behind the first sledge. Although Hanssen, an excellent dog driver whose qualities Amundsen had come to appreciate on the *Gjøa* expedition, had not at first wanted to sail with him on the *Fram*, he managed to change his mind. Hanssen was paid double. The second compass, on the second sledge, was in the charge of Hjalmar Johansen, an experienced man who had travelled in the Arctic with Fridtjof Nansen. Amundsen watched over the third compass, and his sledge was also fitted with a bicycle wheel with a rotation counter to measure the distance they covered. The four men were surprised to find travelling conditions on the ice shelf were similar to those on any other glacier. The average temperature was around minus 12°. Shackleton's reports had led Amundsen to expect great difficulties, so he was pleasantly surprised. Like his companions, he felt as if he were back in the Norwegian mountains. 'We have covered 15 geographical miles ... 11th February. The dogs are pulling splendidly, and travelling conditions on the Barrier are ideal. I don't understand why the English say dogs can't be used here ... 13th February. A lot of loose snow today. The skiing was splendid. But I really don't know how men (on foot) and horses can manage in this kind of snow, let alone a motorised vehicle... . 15th February. Our dogs have done so well – 40 geographical miles yesterday, ten of them with heavy loads, followed by 51 today.'

On 14 February they reached 80 degrees South, at least according to their calculations; Amundsen's theodolite, which could have been used to determine the exact position, was broken. Immediately after setting up the depot, the men set off for home, hoping to return to Framheim before the *Fram* left the Bay of Whales. It took them two days, but they still arrived 12 hours too late. 'It was strange,' Amundsen wrote, 'not to see her there any more. We became melancholy and we felt as though we were lost. But the time would come, I hoped, for us to meet again once our work was successfully completed.'

Other depots were to be placed at 163 degrees West and at 81 and 82 degrees South, and perhaps 83 degrees. Before that, their footwear had to be altered, as it was too tight, causing blisters and encouraging frostbite. 'It looks like a factory here, a flourishing cobblers' establishment. Our enormous skiing boots from Andersen (Christiania) need altering. They have turned out to be too stiff in the cold ... we are trying absolutely everything.' They took the heavy skiing boots apart at the seams and put in leather gussets. Everyone had their own method, but little experience of shoemaking. The men tinkered with their shoes for months on end, trying to come up with better solutions throughout the winter. On 22 February the Norwegians went south again, eight men, seven sledges and 42 dogs, and once again Prestrud went ahead of the convoy, which was lined up as though it were tied together by a thread. Later, he was replaced by the Norwegian skiing champion Olav Bjaaland. When they crept out of their two-man tents on the morning of the third day, they were hit by a snowstorm. 'Until the sun comes up, you never know what sort of day it will be,' was Amundsen's dry reaction, although at that time of the year the sun never sets within the Polar Circle. They packed up their tents and loaded them onto the sledges. As the journey progressed, the dogs began to suffer; five weeks on the ice shelf had not been enough to acclimatize them. Though storms could not harm them, because they lowered an inner eyelid over their eyeballs, like snow goggles – an effective protection against the weather – the skin on the soles of their paws had not yet hardened, so that it had little resistance; and the snow produced sharp-edged cuts in them. In the evening, when the men put up the tents, they had to tend to the huskies' bleeding paws.

On the fifth day they reached the first depot at 80 degrees South. The snowstorm had abated, but the temperature fell to minus 40°. The men were too warmly dressed, and started to sweat when they skied alongside the dog teams. The sweat would condense and freeze, and their outer clothing became coated with hoarfrost. In their tents at night they hung their anoraks, frozen stiff, over the primus stove to make them wearable again the next day.

On 3 March they reached 81 degrees South and set up a second depot. Bjaaland, Hassel and Stubberud returned with the weakest dogs, and the others went on. Sverre Hassel, like Hanssen a brilliant dog driver, had not wanted to take part in the expedition either; he did not see the point of a route which went to the North Pole via South America, exposing the huskies to the heat of the equator two times over. But, for the sake of the dogs, Amundsen had managed to talk him into sailing with the *Fram*, at least as far as San Francisco. Hassel agreed, only to find himself once again in the Antarctic instead of the Californian sun; but he never reproached his chief with this deception.

Amundsen wanted to reach 83 degrees South, but the conditions were becoming extreme – exceptionally hard, even for Norwegians used to the cold. On 6 March Johansen wrote in his diary: 'We covered 16.5 miles today; the last part of the distance seemed to take forever. We had to use the whip on the dogs.' The following day, they only covered 13 miles. 'The chief's dogs are the worst; they no longer pay any attention to the whip, and just lie down.' One of the dogs did not get up again, and froze to death a few hours after he had been put on a sledge. In the evening Johansen chopped up the body with an axe and threw the pieces to the other dogs to eat. Amundsen had planned to feed the animals in this way – canine cannibalism. The weak had to feed the strong, allowing the team to reduce the weight on the sledges and increase their rate of travel. The men did not spare the dogs, and they did not spare themselves. The mercury in the thermometers had long since frozen, and the breath burned in their throats. If their skis loosened or came undone, they had to do them back up with frozen fingers.

The frost blisters on their fingertips burst, and the cold made their faces raw. This trek now bore no resemblance at all to a jolly skiing trip amid the Norwegian mountains. Amundsen walked alongside his sledge, his face twisted with pain, and for days he had been complaining of haemorrhoids and other aches and pains. Every step was a torment, and relieving himself was agonizing. But he did not say a word. He had to reach 83 degrees South to set up the third depot. Otherwise, he thought the whole project would be at risk; and there were still 25 kilometres to go before they reached 82 degrees South. The five men swore quietly and became bad-tempered; they crawled exhausted into their tents, earlier than they had done before. Amundsen had to admit they could not cope any more. 'I have decided to place the depot at 82 degrees South. There is no point in going on any further.' On the following day they completed the final 25 kilometres, one degree less than had been planned; but it was the very most they could manage, 'the utmost that the dogs could endure. The poor animals were exhausted. My one black memory from down there is how worn out those fine dogs were. It was too much to ask of them. The one consolation is that I did not spare myself either'. For the men, the trip was a defeat, a depot journey that cost the lives of eight dogs, a fiasco. Amundsen asked all the men to declare frankly what they thought about it all before they got ready to go back. They sat close together in one of the two-man tents and no-one wanted to be the first to say anything, but then Johansen spoke; it was as if Fridtjof Nansen were talking. The sleeping-bags are no good, he said; when he had been with Nansen in the Arctic ice, he had discovered the value of lined sleeping-bags. This was just what Amundsen had been expecting to hear. 'I have slept in all sorts of tents, and even outdoors, but this tent is the worst of all, and the same goes for the cooking equipment.' Johansen knew what he was talking about. There were two small tents for five men; they cooked in one and ate in the other. 'As a result, meals are pretty much the worst part of the day. We have to carry the food from one tent to the other, so the pemmican got cold before we could eat it. Then we get thirsty, but there is very little water, and it is in the other tent. If we are going to manage the journey to the Pole itself, a lot of things will have to be changed.'

Amundsen let Johansen have his say. He knew he was right, and the tents would be changed. Yet he also felt the other man's arguments were an attack. Johansen certainly had it in him to lead an expedition of his own, and Amundsen saw the shadow of another man behind him. When Nansen had handed over *Fram* to Amundsen, his junior, it was as if he had placed the best man in the ice alongside him like a cuckoo's egg in his nest. In 1896 the world had acclaimed Nansen and Johansen as daring Polar explorers, but later the talk was only of Nansen. But though in Polar regions Hjalmar Johansen was as strong as a bear, the best comrade one could wish for amidst the ice and the cold, he was not fitted for everyday life on dry land. For him the idea of a cosy room, or an office or a marriage, was just oppressive, and his only desire was to leave Norway and return to the clear light of the frozen lands. He was not the first or the only Polar explorer who, when he was not amidst the ice, only felt comfortable in inns where there were always drinking companions ready to listen to the tales of a former hero. He had saved Nansen's life during their trek over the Arctic ice, so Nansen wanted to help put him back on his feet and give him a chance. Amundsen thought this would lead to trouble, but he had been forced to go along with what his patron wanted. A drinker might endanger the whole expedition, but a more significant concern for Amundsen was that Johansen might undermine his own authority. Amundsen knew that there was bound to be trouble between them at some point, and he also had no intention of taking Nansen's man with him to the Pole. But he would need a justification for leaving him out that would not make the men think he was being unfair, and so far Johansen had offered no such justification. 'Amundsen said that from 82 degrees South on, there should be as few men and as many dogs as possible. That was how we would do things.' When Johansen recorded Amundsen's conclusion in his diary, he knew that the latter was right, but he had no idea that he would set off for the Pole without him.

The next morning the men set off for home; it was stormy and cold, minus 30 to 40°. The dogs ran well, and after the discussion, the men seemed transformed. The sky soon turned dark, a sure sign they were now not far from the Ross Sea; the return journey became an easy run on the sledges. Later that afternoon, they Bay of Whales was in sight. 'Everything is exactly as we left it.' Amundsen was relieved.

More than 12 tons of supplies had been transported over 380 kilometres to the south and divided between three depots between 80 and 82 degrees South, enough to feed the dogs for three months, and 110 litres of paraffin, which was more than sufficient to last 200 days. Before the sun disappeared below the horizon for months on end, however, Amundsen wanted to take another ton of seal meat to the first depot, fresh meat for the dogs. If they were to return before the Polar darkness descended, they would have to set off within ten days. Within a week, Hassel and Wisting sewed the two-man tents together to make four and five-man tents. Oscar Wisting had a master's certificate and had sailed on whalers off Iceland; his role in the team was as a sort of first-aid specialist. On Amundsen's recommendation, he had had to complete a number of hospital courses on dentistry and surgery before the voyage. Wisting was just the sort of man Amundsen needed: he was practical, had many talents, and above all he unconditionally accepted the chief's authority.

Once again they loaded up the sledges and the caravan headed southwards back over the white desert of the shelf ice; they also wanted to mark the route more clearly. This time Amundsen, who was still suffering from haemorrhoids, did not come. He handed over command of the crew to Johansen and remained behind in Framheim with the cook Lindstrøm, a man who could still surprise him even after the three years they had spent together on the *Gjøa*, 'a harder-working man there has never been in the Polar regions. It is my profound hope that one day I will be able to do something for him. He has done more and better things for Norwegian Polar exploration than anyone else. If only the good old Norwegians could understand that some day – my God, you have to be thankful for such a crew as this.'

Ten days later the depot party was back – three days sooner than expected. The men had got stuck in a labyrinth of crevasses in the fog, and had lost two dogs. Both of the lead dogs had fallen through a snow hole, snapping the tackle, and they had fallen into the abyss. It had taken them two days to find their way out of the landscape of holes and cracks. As well as a ton of seal meat, they had taken 165 litres of paraffin to 80 degrees South, as well as other useful supplies, so that there were now two tons of provisions there.

Amundsen had reason to be happy with their preparations on the Ross Ice Shelf, and in the history of Antarctic exploration, no attempt to reach the Pole had ever been so thoroughly prepared for. The entire route as far as 80 degrees South was marked out mile after mile with flags and snow pyramids. 'Tomorrow we celebrate the end of our autumn work, and we can do so with a clear conscience. Then it will be Easter, and we can rest for the whole week.' The others had no idea that he had been thinking about Scott and his motorised sledges all week long.

Meanwhile, the British expedition had also been busy with depot journeys in the McMurdo Sound, but without following any precise plan. Just as he had done during the

Discovery expedition, Scott relied on on-the-spot inspiration, but he had neither the talent nor sufficient experience for it. The *Terra Nova* had delivered him from the mild climate of England to the frozen bay, but he had not formulated a practicable plan for the trek to the South Pole. He sent one exploration group west into Victoria Land, and another eastwards on the *Terra Nova* to investigate King Edward VII Land, reserving the southward journey for himself. All he knew about this was what he had read in Shackleton's report on his expedition; he wanted to do better than his rival had. He had unloaded all the equipment he needed to do this onto the White Continent, but the Antarctic is no place for dealing with a lot of equipment. Scott would find this again and again, starting in January 1911, when the ice off Cape Evans collapsed, and the crew struggled to reconstruct their headquarters deeper in the McMurdo Sound, at Hut Point.

Scott's improvisations often amounted to knee-jerk reactions determined by his state of mind. He felt that unexpected bad weather was almost a personal insult, and he saw nature in general as an unpredictable force opposed to mankind. After all, pack ice had prevented the *Terra Nova* from entering the Ross Sea for days on end, and the ice had opened under the first motorised sledge that his men unloaded and swallowed it up. Then there were the attacks of the killer whales with their black and white-patterned heads; hunting for seals, they leaped out of the water onto the ice to make it tip over. The photographer Herbert Ponting narrowly escaped being eaten by them. Ponting was working on the first professional photographic record of the Antarctic, and one morning he had been photographing passing killer whales from the edge of the ice. The whales jumped onto it and slammed into the part where the photographer was standing, so that it broke off. Only Ponting's great agility enabled him to escape from them by leaping from ice floe to ice floe. The geologist Campbell's amused summary of this event was: 'What irony of fate to be eaten by a whale thinking one was a seal and then spat out because one was only a photographer.' But Scott, the leader of the expedition, saw it as yet another sign that he had landed on *terra incognita* in order to subdue nature. This was a further difference from Amundsen, who wanted to conquer the Pole, but not to master its inhospitable geography. He respected the *terra incognita*, but Scott came as a warrior, shielded against the ice, snow and cold by ponies, dogs and motorised sledges as though he and his men were setting out to fight a final battle whose result was already determined before it began.

At the end of January, once both camps, Cape Evans and Hut Point, has been established, Scott informed his men that it was his intention 'to go forward with five weeks' food for men and animals; to depot a fortnight's supply after twelve or thirteen days and return here'. Amundsen meanwhile was placing three depots between 80 and 82 degrees South, but Scott intended to set up just one main depot at 80 degrees South, relying subsequently on supplementary groups to provide assistance and food by accompanying him for part of his journey to the Pole and by coming out to meet him as he returned. It turned out to be a disaster. Gran, who tried in vain to make clear to the Englishmen how useful skis could be in this landscape, wrote in his diary: 'I am convinced of one thing: we will be lucky to reach the Pole next year.' Because Scott thought it was impossible to lead a pony on skis, he ordered Gran, who was a skiing instructor, to pack up his skis on one of the sledges and wade through the snow on foot.

The going was difficult as the convoy made its way southwards to set up the first supply depot. Each morning, the heavily-laden ponies would set off first because they made slower progress than the dogs and the sledges. The animals continually got stuck in fresh snow, and Captain Oates, who was responsible for the horses, had considerable difficulty freeing them from its chilly embrace with the help of the other men. The dogs were sent out later so that they would arrive at the next camp at the same time as the ponies. Every morning their departure was accompanied by confusion and misunderstandings between dog and pony drivers, which Scott struggled to smooth over. His directions and orders would be swept away by the next snowstorm. In storms, the ponies were unable to walk, so that they stood in the snow with their heads to the ground, with no defence against the cold. The men continually rubbed the animals down with straw, but this had long since got wet. While the ponies waited for the storm to pass, the dogs would overtake them, and so the plan for the day fell apart. On many days when a storm set in before their scheduled departure, Scott would order them to stay in their tents and wait for better weather. The temperature rose, bringing either rain or fog to the shelf ice; its moisture penetrated every crack and soaked through the thick coat of the ponies; however often Oates rubbed them down, this could do nothing to cure them of the weakness brought on by hunger, cold and wet. Scott firmly rejected the idea of killing the weakest animals to store in the depot as food for the dogs or the men. After 24 days, at 79 degrees 28 minutes South, both men and animals had reached their limits. Weary Willie, Gran's pony, was now too exhausted to stand up. Oates suggested shooting it and going on to 80 degrees South. 'I'm not going to defy my feelings,' Scott replied, 'just so we can keep going. Regret it or not, my dear Oates, I've made up my mind, like a Christian.' He ordered them to take good care of Weary Willie and to set up the depot there and then. This was a fateful decision that would cost the lives of Scott and other men. Weary Willie died on the return journey.

From Cape Evans, it had taken them four weeks to reach 79 degrees South, where they set up the so-called One Ton Depot, before their intended goal. Amundsen had reached 80 degrees South in five days and was back at Framheim two days after that. The average rate of progress of the English depot journey, divided as it was into dog and pony cohorts, was almost 60 per cent less than what the Norwegian party managed. Thirteen men had struggled for a whole month to transport a ton of supplies close to 80 degrees South, whereas the Norwegians and 50 dogs had succeeded in bringing two tons of supplies two degrees further south. Gran wrote in his diary: 'Our team is divided and we resemble a defeated, disappointed, disconsolate army.'

Scott knew nothing of Amundsen's depot journeys, but even if he had he would not have altered his own strategy in any way. He firmly believed that dogs could not sustain the journey over the ice shelf and the glaciers, and nothing could change his mind. What was more, rather than thinking about Amundsen, Scott was inclined to compare himself with Shackleton, his true rival. If he could surpass him he would reach the Pole, and complete Shackleton's journey. All that mattered was how far they got, not how fast they went. There is no clearer indication of Scott's refusal to enter into a contest for the Pole with Amundsen.

Weary Willy was not the only pony to die during Scott's depot journey. Seven animals died – seven out of eight. Once they had reached Hut Point, the encampment used on the *Discovery* expedition, breaking ice prevented them from getting back to Cape Evans. Once again, Scott felt that nature was conspiring against him, and he had to wait for the sea to freeze over. His time as a cadet at Dartmouth had not taught him how to wait, and Scott was both bad-tempered and nervous. 'I am impatient of our wait here. But I shall be impatient also in the main hut. It is ill to sit still and contemplate the ruin which has assailed our transport. The Pole is a long way off, alas!' He waited three weeks with his men at Hut Point, and then he could stand it no longer, and threw himself into a senseless struggle with nature. He ordered them to proceed over the thin autumn ice to Cape Evans, gambling with the solidity of the existing ice cover and the force of the wind, which could have blown the crew into the sea. The men were lucky, and survived – but only by a whisker.

On 21 April 1911, the sun set over Framheim for the next four months; everyone in the camp knew what he had to do. At 7.30 a.m. Lindstrøm would wake the others up to eat breakfast together, and they began working at nine, with a two-hour break for lunch at 11.30. 'We usually have plenty to discuss; and even if not, there is nothing depressing about silence. We like it, and find it refreshing not to talk.' After two o'clock, they went back to work until 5.15, a total of 7¼ hours per day, six days a week. At 8 a.m., midday and 8 p.m. meteorological data were recorded, although not at night, which put the scientific value of these observations in doubt. 'Our single goal is to reach the Pole, and everything else has to take second place. If we made a measurement during the night, the lights would have to be kept on continuously. As we have only one room, that would disturb most of us and so be detrimental for all. My main concern is that every aspect of our lives during the winter should be conducted sensibly. We have to eat and sleep well so that when spring arrives, we are in a good state mentally and physically, and so we can struggle to reach the goal that we must attain at all costs.'

This one room, though, was carpeted, and they only entered it wearing socks; pictures hung on the walls, together with the Norwegian flag and some postcards. There was plenty of room for each man's bed and locker. The base camp was kept at a comfortable 20° by an oil heating system, one of civilization's latest achievements. Framheim was to be a model for later Antarctic stations. Various food and equipment stores and workshops were connected to the living section by a system of tunnels dug out of the ice and snow, and this also provided access to the round snowproof tents in which the dogs were kept. There was also a bathroom and a toilet that was very easy to keep clean. 'Admittedly, we have no water, but on the other hand there are the dogs, who dispose of the night soil quickly and completely.' A shaft leading to the surface gave the huskies, their garbage disposal system, free access to the cesspit. More than one hundred dogs kept it clean. Amundsen understood perfectly how to exploit natural processes that he observed.

The Norwegian party spent four months in this system of snow trenches and ice tunnels, but they had plenty to keep them occupied. The boots were overhauled once more, and also some of their clothing; the tents were sealed at the bottom – yet another Framheim innovation. The sledges were too heavy as they were, so their runners and other wooden components were sanded down, reducing their weight from 50 kilograms to just 35. A second pair of skis was made for each man. There was plenty for them to do to prepare the equipment for the trek to the Pole as best they knew how, and the inhabitants of the base camp did not mind that the temperature on the shelf ice fell below minus 50 each night. Every morning, Lindstrøm served hot pancakes with bottled blueberries and cloudberries, the traditional

Norwegian remedy against scurvy. Twice a day, for lunch and dinner, they ate seal, cooked so as to be both tasty and nutritious. Throughout the winter, Amundsen's crew built up a reserve of Vitamin C; they ate wholemeal bread fortified with grains of wheat and leavened with fresh yeast. The food was simple, but nutritious and natural. All this was determined by the great goal of reaching the South Pole before the British party.

The atmosphere in Framheim was good, even friendly, and Johansen's criticisms seemed to have been forgotten. Towards the end of the Polar winter, however, Amundsen became impatient, as though he could not wait for the spring. Sverre Hassel knew why: 'The thought of the Englishmen tormented him. For if we don't get there first, we might just as well have stayed at home.' Amundsen began to be annoyed by trivialities; sometimes he jumped up and down on the ice to test the firmness of the shelf, or he would go outside because he imagined he heard the sound of motorised sledges. His diary is full of references to Shackleton, but really he was thinking about Scott. '11th July – either the English expedition had bad dogs, or they did not know how to manage them ... if Shackleton had been appropriately equipped, with dogs, furs and above all with skis, the South Pole chapter would already have been closed. I have the utmost admiration for what he and his men managed to achieve given the equipment they had. They had courage, persistence and strength aplenty. Just a bit more experience – such as a journey through the far harder arctic ice – and their efforts would have been rewarded with success. The English have told the whole world loud and clear that skis and dogs are useless in these regions, and that furs are no good. We shall see.'

The Norwegians were astonished to find that their leader was beginning to doubt everything; he overreacted to trivialities, and kept himself to himself. Amundsen was in the midst of a personal crisis with only one possible resolution: to set off for the Pole. He could hardly wait.

At the other end of the Great Ice Barrier, at Cape Evans, tensions between the men were growing, and Scott had lost his constant smile. Although, as Gran said, the party was living a life 'replete with things regarded as luxuries even in civilization', every meal was overshadowed by an uninvited guest. One man said what all the others were thinking: 'Amundsen's chances are significantly better than our own. They are 60 miles nearer to the Pole than we are and they can make straight for the Pole, whereas we have to go round the islands first.' All of them apart from Scott. 'I would like to repeat once again that this expedition makes its plans and does its work as if Amundsen did not exist.'

Teddy Evans, who had saved the *Terra Nova*, suggested concentrating all the expedition's energies on the South Pole instead of sending individual parties west or east to carry out scientific research. He said that England wanted to see the King's flag planted at the Pole. Not a bad idea, but Scott reacted to it as though it were an attempted mutiny, rejecting any suggestion from a subordinate; he had been sent to explore an unknown continent, not just to march south. Nonetheless, it was a march on which his promotion depended. He would become a rear admiral if all went well and he was the first to reach the Pole.

Scott increasingly withdrew into the command structures of the Royal Navy. The distance between him and the men increased, as did his isolation. The hut at Cape Evans was divided into two messes, one for officers and one for the men, by a wall of packing cases, which made it impossible for a common team spirit to develop. Scott also made less use of the winter months for necessary preparations, leaving the men more or less to themselves. They played football, as they had done on the *Discovery*, wrote a 'South Polar Times', and met at night for discussion groups on all sorts of subjects, very few of which had anything to do with polar exploration. In this 'Universitas Antarctica' he occasionally recovered his smile, and regained a certain respect amongst the scientists. 'There is no specialist here who is not pleased to discuss his problems with him.' But the commander of the British expedition did not talk about the realities of ice, snow and cold.

On 27 June a small group led by the zoologist Wilson set off on a research trip to collect the egg of an Emperor Penguin at a certain stage of development; once again, Scott accompanied them. The pulled the sledges themselves because none of them knew how to use skis, and on some days they only managed to go one or two miles. After five weeks at temperatures of minus 40 or 50°, they turned back with the egg; their clothes were frozen solid. 'One continues to wonder as to the possibilities of fur clothing as made by the Esquimeaux, with a sneaking feeling that it may outclass our more civilised garb. For us this can only be a matter of speculation, as it would have been quite impossible to have obtained such articles,' wrote Scott in his diary. On 9 September Teddy Evans, Tryggve Gran and the seaman Forde set off on a small depot journey, and once again the men hauled their sledges. During one unbroken 24-hour stretch, they made 63 kilometres. Scott too put himself in harness for a trip to the western mountains, pulling a sledge around 270 kilometres through the snow to the west and back with three companions. Not everyone understood their commander's interest in photographing the glacier formations of Victoria Land. 'It is not quite clear why they are going or what they are going to do,' one diary entry comments.

On 10 September, Captain Scott announced his final plan for the conquest of the South Pole. He wanted to be back at Cape Evans with his team by the middle of March, a date perilously near the beginning of the Polar winter. Amundsen was planning to return to Framheim by the beginning of January, late summer. Scott's timetable did not allow sufficient safety margins, but nobody contradicted him. 'Everyone was enthusiastic. Although people have given a good deal of thought to various branches of the subject, there was not a suggestion offered for improvement. The scheme seems to have earned full confidence: it remains to play the game out.'

But the result was already decided.

Captain Scott sits at the head of the table for his birthday celebration at Cape Evans, 6 June 1911. Captain Oates stands on the left of the photograph.

8

The Route, or the Fine Art of Pragmatism

'It's good to make a show ... to continue the British tradition of exploration and prove that our old spirit of adventure is still alive.'

Captain Scott

'A number of people seem to be outraged by what we are doing down here – a breach of etiquette? Are these people mad? Is the Pole Scott's and Scott's alone? I don't care what these fools think.'

Roald Amundsen

Amundsen could not overcome his disquiet. The British motor sledges hummed in his head, giving him no peace. He was trapped like a tiger in a cage, long since ready to make his leap. He wanted to set off for 83 degrees South earlier than planned and build igloos there and wait for the midnight sun before attempting to advance into the unknown King Edward VII Land and test out their equipment.

His suggestions were discussed and rejected, and then he made a final decision. When the sun returned on 24 August, they would set off. He did not permit any further discussion of this early departure date. Johansen, who had polar experience, warned: 'We cannot start while the temperature remains so low.' In recent weeks, the temperature had not risen above minus 50°. But Amundsen asserted his authority and had seven sledges prepared for departure. He was the boss. On 24 August the sun rose above the horizon, barely making its presence felt in the cloudy sky. It remained cold. Finally, on 31 August, the thermometer rose to minus 26°, but a storm blew the snow against the men at a speed of 23 knots. Once again they had to wait. Then the storm abated and the temperature fell to minus 46°. Johansen wrote: 'It's a good thing we're here indoors and not a few miles above the barrier, unable to go a step further; then all might be lost at the start, around 80 degrees South; a terrible beginning.' When the temperature rose to minus 27°, Amundsen was unstoppable.

On 8 September 1911 at ten past twelve, eight men with seven sledges and 86 dogs between them set off on the last great adventure in the history of the exploration of the Earth, leaving Lindstrøm behind in Framheim on his own. It was too early, but the convoy still made good progress in the next few days, as if they were on a Sunday outing in Norway. There was no need to use the whip, as the dogs were in high spirits after the winter months. Occasionally the men had to take one or two of the dogs out of their teams and tie them behind the sledges for braking, in order to reduce their speed. A bitch went on heat and was shot 'for moral turpitude', because she would throw the dog teams into disarray.

Amundsen was pleased with their average rate of progress of 28 kilometres per day. The night before the third day the temperature fell nearly 30° to minus 56°, but still the sledge teams managed to cover 28 kilometres. The breath of men and dogs froze instantaneously into beads of ice around their lips and noses. The convoy was veiled in thick white mist, so that the man at the front became invisible. Amundsen now knew that they had started too soon, and did not want to admit it to himself – not yet. As long as he and his men kept up with the dogs, they felt warm in their Eskimo clothing: wolfskin anoraks and reindeer-skin underclothes. Nonetheless, the cold consumed their energy to the core, and they longed to stop for the night. But the conditions were terrible, and they could not sleep. 'The hoarfrost made everything damp. God knows how it will all end.' They tossed and turned in their sleeping bags, which afforded no protection against the cold. Nobody slept a wink, but the nights passed in silence, except when one man had to step over his neighbour's clammy, freezing sleeping bag to go outside, accompanied by earthy curses. Amundsen could hear the swearing, even in the next tent, and he realised that something had to be done – that very morning. They struggled to harness the dogs, many of which had frostbitten paws, making them rebellious. They snapped at the drivers, who had to use their whips to get them ready to set off. The men's clothes were frozen solid and their boots were tight with the cold until they had been walked in. The men were exhausted by the night and listless; they did not look like victors. Nonetheless, they set off. It was the fifth day. The mercury in the thermometers froze, and Prestrud's toes were raw from the cold. After 7 kilometres they gave up trying to spur the dogs on and stopped. They built two igloos, because no-one wanted to crawl into the tents. Inside, they drank hot chocolate, and this made them warm enough to talk again. Bjaaland wrote: 'Amundsen's mood is at rock bottom, and he has decided to return to the camp, quite rightly, or else we would all have frozen to death.' Amundsen felt his responsibility for his companions, and was forced to admit to himself that Johansen had been right: it was too early to set off for the Pole. But he did not say so, and even his diary fails to mention that this had been his decision alone. 'There is no question of risking the lives of the men and the dogs out of mere stubbornness by going on just because we have decided to start. If we want to win, each stone must be carefully laid – one false move and all may be lost.'

They turned back, and on 14 September they were once more at the 80 degree depot. They left all their equipment there and continued with almost empty sledges. Bjaaland wrote: 'It was a pretty chilly business sledging at 55–56 degrees below.' Amundsen had a bottle of Dutch gin in his bag that he had been saving for a more cheerful occasion, but he decided to open it to raise their spirits. But the bottle had burst, its contents frozen. '15th September: minus

47.5 degrees, and on top of that a north-west wind in our faces.' The dogs suffered as much as the men. They were in a miserable condition, their paws swollen with frostbite so that every step became a torment. Some of the dogs were too exhausted to dig a hole in the snow to lie in, and they froze to death on the ground. Others were too weak to pull properly and had to be carried on the sledges. On 16 September, the temperature was slightly higher, minus 44°, and the team felt that they had got away with it again – as long as the temperature held, and did not fall again during the remaining 72 kilometres. Amundsen ordered them to go straight to Framheim without stopping. When they set off at seven o'clock, he took Wisting's sledge with the strongest dogs, and the two men raced off together with Hanssen's team, terrified of the next cold front. Soon they had disappeared over the horizon to the north, and the others could not keep up with them. Amundsen left his comrades in the lurch like a captain deserting his sinking ship. 'This caused bad feeling,' Johansen wrote in his diary. 'We were gloomy and felt that something had gone dreadfully wrong. All of a sudden, we were no longer happy and cheerful.' Nine hours later, Amundsen, Wisting and Hanssen were back at Framheim. The weather was calm and sunny. Meanwhile the other men out on the Ross Barrier were already struggling to survive against the onslaught of the cold, each man thinking only of himself.

Stubberud could still see the three men in the distance for a while, but his dogs could not keep up and he stopped, sitting on his sledge to wait for the others. He knew that he would be finished if there was a snowstorm, with no primus stove and no tent. He ate his last ship's biscuit. Then Bjaaland appeared, at the head of his team of dogs. Stubberud joined him and they reached the base camp two hours after Amundsen. Shortly after that Hassel arrived at Framheim, and all he knew of the two remaining men, Johansen and Prestrud, was that they were a long way behind and had no fuel or food. As the weather worsened, the men looked at Amundsen to see what he would do, but he could not make up his mind to go back to meet them. 'Johansen is a veteran polar explorer, and he will set up a camp and keep going the next day,' he said. They were a long way behind.

Confronted the following morning by the raging storm, Johansen knew that Prestrud was behind him with the weakest dogs, and he felt somehow responsible for him. When he saw that Prestrud's team was getting weaker and weaker, he attempted to catch up with Hassel, who was ahead of him. It took him six hours. He was furious and asked Hassel to wait for Prestrud with him, but Hassel refused. 'I did not have a stove or any paraffin, or cooking equipment, and the situation would have been just the same whether there were three of us or only two.' He gave him his tent and raced ahead while Johansen waited for Prestrud, so saving his life.

Two hours later Prestrud staggered up, his feet badly frostbitten and aching. He was profoundly exhausted, and Johansen barely managed to stop him from lying down in the snow. The two men went on together, hour after hour, an endless torment. The worst thing was not their hunger or the increasingly bitter temperatures, but the agonising feeling that they had been left in the lurch by their comrades. Prestrud and Johansen reached Framheim half an hour after midnight; Lindstrøm had waited up for them, and had hot chocolate ready. Amundsen was not inclined to listen to Johansen's accusations – what could he have said in his defence? Like the others, he lay in his bunk and went to sleep, relieved. The Polar team had all got back safely.

The next morning at breakfast, he asked why Johansen had got back so late. He did not ask Prestrud, he asked Johansen. He knew that it was Johansen he had to sort things out with, not Prestrud. Johansen exploded, giving vent to his feelings. 'This isn't an expedition, it's a nightmare! A leader shouldn't leave his men behind.' Everyone round the table knew that Johansen was right, and agreed with him, but they did not say so. The disagreement was between Johansen and the boss, and now it was out in the open. Amundsen took the other man's words as mutiny, which was not Johansen's intention, and his face grew hard. The unforgivable thing about what Johansen had said, Amundsen later explained, was that 'he spoke in front of everybody. It was necessary to grasp the bull by the horns; I had to set an example.'

He talked to the other men individually to assure himself of their loyalty, and gave Johansen his decision in writing: 'For the sake of the success of the expedition, the only thing to do is to exclude you from the journey to the South Pole.'

Instead, Johansen was to undertake a journey to King Edward VII Land under the command of Prestrud. He replied to this decision likewise in writing: 'The leader of the expedition has decided to put me under the command of a younger man who will be undertaking such a task for the first time. It must be clear that this is humiliating for someone who has spent a considerable part of his life in the ice.' This was just what Amundsen wanted to achieve – to humiliate Johansen, his rival for the leadership of the expedition, and to subject him to his own authority. Prestrud gave up the South Pole with no regrets, as he felt he was not up to the rigours of the journey. Once Amundsen had managed to convince his carpenter Stubberud that he needed him as a reliable man to go with Johansen, so that the trip to King Edward VII Land would be undertaken by a team of three, there was nothing for it but for Johansen to obey.

For a while it had looked as if Amundsen might lose control of the expedition, but at a stroke he was once more fully in charge; he had assured the loyalty of his men and pushed Johansen aside, as well as reducing the Polar team from eight men to five, so nearly doubling his food supply. What was more, he had made sure that if he did not reach the South Pole, Norwegians would be the first men to set foot in the land at the eastern end of the Ross Ice Barrier. Here he was counting on Johansen's Polar obsession. He knew what the latter was capable of achieving, and so he had kicked him out, because he had always perceived Johansen's abilities as a challenge to his own authority. Now he stopped speaking to him. 'He behaves as though I did not have anything to do with the expedition. He is wounded to the quick because his role as leader is under threat. He is not the man I thought he was, and he is not up to leading an expedition like this one,' wrote Johansen. Amundsen had managed to snatch victory out of the jaws of defeat, but at the cost 'of bringing our wonderful unity of purpose to this sad end'.

The temperature gradually rose to minus 20°, and a petrel was sighted flying over Framheim, a sure sign of the approach of spring. They wanted to set off on 15 October; both the huskies and the men had recovered, and they made further improvements to their boots. Bjaaland wrote: 'So we are ready to go once more. I hope it won't be a fiasco like last time. If I make it back from this journey, I will have to give up polar exploration. It isn't worth all the trouble – and if something out there gets me, well, my very best wishes to my friends and acquaintances, my fellow Norwegians and my fatherland.'

Then they set off again – Amundsen, Bjaaland, Wisting, Hassel and Hanssen. Prestrud filmed the occasion. The expression on Johansen's face is not recorded, nor the little scene in which Amundsen went up to the older man to take his leave of him with a handshake as he had already done from Stubberud and Lindstrøm. Johansen wished him luck and went back into the hut: 'I told him the truth, and that is not always pleasant to hear; so I fell out of favour. I think I have been of some use to him; now we have parted. One sledge after the other set off, over the ice, over the bay and up onto the barrier. By midday they were all at the top, and then they set off on the old path we know so well.'

It was 20 October 1911. The gloomy atmosphere that had recently prevailed at Framheim was replaced by joyful expectation. Those who were racing southward with their dog teams all acknowledged the authority of one man, Amundsen, who could rely on a resolute team, though a smaller one. Every man was first class. He could not have found a better group.

The weather failed to live up to its promise, and the crew ran into a violent storm, followed by fog. They wandered off the marked path on the very first day, ending up in a field of crevasses. 'Roald Amundsen was next to me on the sledge. We sat back to back. Suddenly the sledge received a hard knock. It seemed as if it was being pressed down behind, with the front end in the air, being pulled backwards. I turned round in a flash and saw that we had driven over an enormous crevasse. When we were half way across, the snow bridge had broken off beneath us; but fortunately, because we were travelling so fast and steadily, the sledge had slid on forwards onto solid ice. We did not stop, but just kept on going. Then Amundsen tapped me on the shoulder. "Did you see that?" he asked. "That would have liked to get every-thing – us two, the sledge and the dogs as well." We said no more about it.'

They were fast, and they were travelling light, at least as far as the first depot. Just as they had had to do on their first abortive attempt, they took some of the dogs out of their traces and carried the extra weight on the sledges. Four dogs that had got too fat at Framheim were removed from their teams and left to fend for themselves – they would find the way back home. The Norwegians raced southwards with 48 dogs, 12 for each sledge; they made 36 kilometres a day. Once they had got out of the field of crevasses, even in the fog they had no trouble finding the path they had marked to 80 degrees South; they arrived there on the fourth day. 'A splendid trial result,' Amundsen said, 'as regards both the milometer on the sledge and the compass.' Now the real adventure would begin, but first they rested up, letting the dogs eat their fill of seal meat. Tomorrow they would load the sledges, harness the dogs and go on. It was 24 October, the very same day the English expedition began their trek to the South Pole. But the Norwegian depot at 80 degrees South was 270 kilometres nearer the Pole than the base camp at Cape Evans. Scott was already four or five days' march behind Amundsen before he had even set off.

Since 10 o'clock two motorised sledges, each with a load of one and a half tons, had been struggling over the sea ice above Hut Point. Evans was in charge of the advance party; Scott intended to follow it a week later with the ponies and some dog sledges. Meanwhile, he and his men wrote their farewell letters. 'My dear ... I am quite on my feet now. I feel both mentally and physically fit for the work, and I realise that the others know it and have full confidence in me. But it is a certain fact that it was not so in London or indeed until after we reached this spot. The root of the trouble was that I had lost confidence in myself ... it is significant of my recovery that I do not allow anxieties to press on me where I deem my actions to have been justified.' Scott's letters continually pit himself against Amundsen, a comparison he concealed from the members of the expedition. He also revealed to Kathleen his fear that Amundsen might reach the Pole first, 'because he is bound to travel fast with dogs and pretty certain to start early. – On this account, I decided at a very early date to act exactly as I should have done had he not existed. Any attempt to race must have wrecked my plan, beside which it doesn't appear the sort of thing one is out for.' To Joseph Kinsey, his New Zealand agent, he wrote that 'if Amundsen gets to the Pole, he is bound to do it with dogs, but one guesses that success will justify him, and that our venture will be out of it. If he fails, he ought to hide! Anyway, he is taking a big risk, and perhaps deserves his luck if he gets through. But he is not there yet!' Scott did not know that Amundsen was already on his way. He still thought approaching the Pole on a broad front, with motor power, ponies, dogs and the resilience of British sailors, was more likely to be successful. 'I'm not a great believer in dog transport beyond a certain point.' Writing to Admiral Egerton, he said, 'Everything depends on the coming journey, of course.'

Oates, like many at Cape Evans, did not share this confidence. 'I expect they have started for the Pole by this, and have a jolly good chance of getting there if their dogs are good and they use them properly. From what I see I think it would not be difficult to get to the Pole provided you have proper transport but with the rubbish we have it will be jolly difficult and mean a lot of hard work.' His letters to his mother also pass judgement on Scott's qualities as a leader. 'Although we got on very well together I dislike Scott intensely and would chuck the thing if it was not that we are the British expedition and must beat the Norwegians. Scott has always been very civil to me and I have the reputation of getting on with him. But the fact of the matter is he is not straight, it is himself first, the rest nowhere, and when he has got what he can out of you, it is shift for yourself.'

On 1 November at eleven o'clock in the morning the main party set out from Cape Evans with eight ponies. Scott was nervous; he harnessed his pony to the wrong sledge, put the mistake right and followed his men hastily over the sea ice towards Hut Point. A few hours later the telephone at Cape Evans rang. The British expedition had laid the first working telephone cable in the Antarctic between the two camps. In all the excitement of the departure Scott had forgotten to bring the Union Jack that Queen Alexandra had given him for the Pole, and he sent Gran back to fetch it. When Gran returned with the flag, Scott's old smile was back. 'The irony of fate, it was a Norwegian who carried the British flag the first few miles towards the Pole.' Five days later the pony party found the motorised sledges, which had broken down just before Corner Camp, at the point where their route – which went to the east at first – turned sharply southwards. 'Our great dream of help from machines is over.'

But there was no sign of Teddy Evans and his team, nor of the supplies themselves.

Later generations cite the failure of the motorised sledges as a symbol of Scott's catastrophic planning of the expedition. A lot of money had been spent on developing them, yet they had taken with them neither the development engineer Skelton, nor the necessary spare parts, nor suitable tools. Scott's much celebrated, energetic approach of taking decisions on the spot had turned out to be an arrogant miscalculation. A product of the old spirit of the already outdated Victorian world view, Scott too believed that manliness and an iron will were typical British virtues that were sufficient in themselves to move mountains. Ever since he had left the Antarctic on the *Discovery*, he had known that he would return to the White Continent – he had had four years to prepare for the expedition, but he had made poor use of them. When he entered the McMurdo Sound for the second time in the *Terra Nova*, Scott was just as bad at skiing as he had been before, and he still favoured the use of equipment that had been shown to be inadequate in the days of the *Discovery*. He still did not wear an anorak or furs, preferring the extreme-weather clothing of the Royal Navy, a waterproof jacket with a button-on hood; he still swore by navy tents that were erected on a metal framework and did not have a fixed bottom, making them almost impossible to put up in stormy conditions. Dartmouth had not taught him to learn from experience; instead, his education led him to believe that a subject of the British Crown could land on his feet anywhere in the world. He was finding it hard in the Antarctic.

On 7 November a snowstorm swept over the ice shelf, and the group stayed in their tents to wait for better weather. Late that morning the sound of barking could be heard in their encampment; Meares was approaching with the dog teams. Cecil Meares was involved in dubious dealings with the Chinese and the Russians on behalf of the Secret Service, and Scott had commissioned him to buy the Siberian dogs. He was amazed that dogs could run in a snowstorm, and in any case he had not been expecting their arrival. According to his timetable, the dogs were supposed to catch up with Scott's ponies and the motorised sledges. Meares and the Russian dog handler Dmetri Girev, whom he had persuaded to join the expedition, had kept exactly to the timetable, but the ponies and motorised sledges had not. Scott was annoyed and gave Meares a dressing-down for meeting him too early, noting that Meares had 'played too much for safety in catching us so soon, but it is satisfactory to find the dogs can be driven to face such a wind as we have had'. Captain Oates, on the other hand, wrote: 'We both damned the motors. 3 motors at £1000 each, 19 ponies at £5 each. 32 dogs at 30/- each. If Scott fails to get to the Pole, he jolly well deserves it. Scott realises now what awful cripples our ponies are and carries a face like a tired seaboot in consequence.' A few days later Scot said in passing to Cherry-Garrard that 'he thought they did everything wrong with their dogs'.

On 21 November the main party found the former motor

group. 'My dear Teddy, always the same', Scott said to his deputy when they met. Evans had had all the cargo from the broken-down sledges unloaded onto the other sledges, and hauled them with his men to the appointed meeting place. They had been waiting for Scott for a week, and they built a 15-foot high snow pyramid to help pass the time. 'My dear Teddy, always the same.' So it was decided. Teddy Evans, who had saved the men from shipwreck off New Zealand, would not join the Polar party. Scott was sure of that, but he still had to tell Teddy Evans.

21 November 1911: 775 kilometres away from Framheim and some 460 kilometres to the south of Scott's current position, Amundsen wrote in his travel diary: 'It was an utter marvel today – the dogs managed 17 miles and a 5000 foot ascent. I dare anyone to say that dogs cannot be employed here.' As every evening, he was the first man in the tent, ready to cook supper for everyone. 'I put the primus on faster than usual and got it going at full blast. I wanted to make as much racket as I could, so I wouldn't be able to hear the shots that would be fired shortly. It was hard, but it had to be. We had agreed that we would stop at nothing to attain our goal. The first shot rang out. I am not nervous, but I have to admit I was startled. Then came one shot after another – a terrible noise in the solitude. With every shot, a faithful servant lost his life. The celebratory mood there should have been in the tent that evening, our first on the plateau, came to nothing. Depression and gloom lay in the air; we had grown fond of the dogs. We called the spot the Butchers' Shop.'

Twenty-seven of the huskies were shot. After they had been skinned, the other eighteen dogs gorged themselves on their fellows. Fresh dog meat would reduce the danger of scurvy, Amundsen said, and this convinced his comrades, although the men did not find it easy cutting out the best pieces of meat from the dogs' bodies for themselves. 'We enjoyed the wonderful dinners of our good Greenlanders,' Bjaaland remembered, 'I must say they tasted excellent.' They spent four days at the Butchers' Shop, at the half-way point between Framheim and the South Pole; time enough for all five men to recall once again their route onto the continental ice mass.

Their average daily rate of progress had been between 25 and 35 kilometres, and they had been on their skis for five or sometimes six hours a day. Even if it was snowy or foggy, it became a responsibility accepted by all to complete the agreed daily stretch: a quarter of a degree per day, according to Amundsen's plan and they would cover a whole degree every four days. This made the endless whiteness of the shelf ice less depressing, because the men could see their progress towards the Pole on an imaginary globe.

Scott measured his approach to the Pole according to the number of miles that still remained to be covered in this inhospitable land of snow and ice. But each of Scott's companions felt differently about every mile of the route, every step taken. If one man's boots were too tight and his feet were getting sore or his toes had frozen, the thought of the last mile before setting up camp would become a torment, perhaps leading him to ask what was the point of his pain or what business the British Empire had in the Antarctic. Scott wrote: 'I was not expecting these marches to be altogether easy, but I had absolutely no idea they would turn out to be as bad as today. Very bad visibility again and very hard ground. After a day like this one, everyone feels bad.'

Amundsen on the other hand had employed the psychological trick of projecting the lines of longitude and latitude onto the frozen waste, as it were using it to bind his men to his leadership. So it was that they made their way as conquering heroes to the imaginary dot of the Pole, where all the lines of longitude coincide, the imaginary end of the Earth. The Norwegians wanted to conquer this point, and they selected the most direct route, straight down the line of 163 degrees West to the south all the way to the end, irrespective of what they were faced with on the way. For Amundsen, there were no detours; he marched straight to his destination. This was the most elegant solution, but not the easiest. They drove their dogs across a great area full of crevasses because it lay on their route and Amundsen did not want to waste time going round it. 'These crevasses are impressive when you look down over the edge. A bottomless abyss which changes from light blue to pitch black'. He was constantly mindful of the British competition, and perhaps that was why he was putting all his money on one horse, the most direct route, and stuck to it through thick and thin. And he was lucky. So far. 'The worst formations we have come across here are holes enormous enough to take the

Fram and to spare. These holes are covered over with a thin crust, and the small opening that is visible appears harmless. But if you end up on top of it, you have had it. We went past one today, but fortunately Helmer Hanssen saw it in time. There is hardly anything that escapes his sharp eyes. We are all well. The risks we are taking when we journey through these thankless zones! Every day we are taking responsibility once more for our lives. But it's good to know that no-one wants to turn back.'

In spite of the fog they managed to find the last depot, the one they had set up at 82 degrees South before the winter. 'It was an absolute triumph. We have demonstrated that it is possible to set up depots amidst these great distances and to mark them in such a way that they can be found again with careful navigation.' Amundsen suggested placing another depot at every succeeding degree instead of taking all their baggage with them to the Pole itself, as originally planned.

'7th November – two o'clock. We have passed 82 degrees 17 minutes South, the *Discovery* expedition's furthest south.' Ahead of them lay some 900 kilometres of unknown territory. 'We are running like greyhounds over this endless flat expanse of snow; the longer the landscape stays the same, the better.' The surface of the ice sheet remained smooth, and the men agreed to increase their daily quota, covering one degree in three days instead of four. 'We have always easily covered the daily quota of twenty miles in five hours. Including the building of the pyramids [the depots] that comes to six and a half hours. This makes for long nights.

The dogs do not seem to be finding it too much. They are a bit thinner, but in better form than ever.' On 11 November the line of the horizon ahead of them broke up into glittering pyramids. 'Brilliant white, shining blue, pitch black – the land looks like something out of a fairy tale. Peak after peak, rock after rock – it is as wild and jagged as anything on this Earth, no-one has seen it before, no-one set foot there. We are going to have to climb up it. It feels wonderful to be travelling here.' Four days later they stood at the craggy transition from the Ross Ice Shelf to the Antarctic continent. Ahead of them lay a chain of mountains about 4,000 metres in height, clad in snow and ice; Amundsen named it the Queen Maud Range in honour of his queen. The Transantarctic Mountains ran over 3,600 kilometres from Cape Adare to the Pensacola Mountains, blocking the outflow of the great ice cap covering the surface of the continent to the sea. Amundsen was confronted with a massive, incredibly craggy dam. Scott followed Shackleton's route through the mountains up to the ice cap, whereas Amundsen had to find his own way in unknown territory. With the agreement of his companions, he changed his strategy once more to fit in with the circumstances. His plan was to make the ascent with all the dogs, and then kill all but 18 of them, who would accompany the men to the Pole; there he would kill six more and complete the return journey with the remaining 12 dogs.

On 18 November 'the terrible ascent finally began'. In fact it was a continual series of ascents and descents – a torment for both men and animals. Often all the huskies had to be teamed up to just one of the sledges to cope with the slope – 'Today the dogs have worked harder then I ever expected them to do' – or else cloths had to be wrapped round the runners to act as brakes and so bring the descent of the sledges under control. After conquering one pass, then a second and a third, followed by a series of little glaciers, making their way further into the mountains all the time, they were faced by a new and humbling challenge, 'a gigantic, enormous glacier just like a fjord running straight across our line of travel from east to west; we are surrounded by a terrible chaos of crevasses in the glacier. Our path is blocked on every side by gigantic blocks of ice, monstrous abysses and wide crevasses', a tremendous glacier flowing from the edge of the polar plateau down to the ice barrier, with a slope of 2,250 metres in just under 14 kilometres. The scenery impressed Amundsen, who wrote: 'Abyss after abyss, crevasse after crevasse, gigantic blocks of ice scattered everywhere. You can certainly see that nature is at its most powerful in this place. It is not without satisfaction that we looked on this spot. We felt that we were strong.' Wisting wrote: 'I have never heard him say: let's turn round.' On 21 November, after they had conquered the Axel Heiberg Glacier (named after one of Amundsen's sponsors), the Norwegian party camped on the edge of the ice cap – one of the greatest achievements in Polar exploration. They had been lucky, and they had achieved a *tour de force*; at an altitude of 3,340 metres, they rested for four days before continuing with 18 huskies. The Norwegian expedition was 460 kilometres ahead of Scott.

The British team, 16 strong, began each day with five staggered departures. First went those of the men who hauled their own sledges, as they made the slowest progress through the snow on top of the shelf ice. Then came the three pony teams, with the horses arranged in order of strength; only after them did the dog-drawn sledges set off. The intention was for all three parties to reach the planned camp for the night at about the same time. Scott's route timetable did little to promote cohesion between the three groups, each of which had to struggle through the day independently before the evening's rest. If the dog drivers paused for a rest during the day, they did not have to look after their animals. The dogs could more or less take care of themselves, but the ponies froze if they stood still, their sweat turning into a coat of ice. Then they had to be rubbed down and covered up, and to protect them from the wind the men had to dig a wall of snow. Many special operations were required in the three groups that could mess up the best-planned timetable again and again. In this way they crossed the ice shelf day after day, sinking up to their knees in the snow, their skis packed on the sledges. The ponies also broke through the snow, and their races became sore. The average speed of the British expedition was more than two kilometres an hour slower than that of the Norwegians, from two to four kilometres an hour.

Scott's transportation system relied on a single depot, One Ton Camp, where additional food and fuel was to be brought out from Cape Evans before his return from the

Pole, and on auxiliary groups accompanying the main party. Once their sledges were empty because the supplies had been used up or been placed in a depot for the return journey, they turned back. On 24 November at about 81 degrees 15 minutes South, the first auxiliary group was sent back to the base camp at Cape Evans. Scott was about 945 kilometres away from the Pole, still on the ice shelf. The first pony was shot, its job done, 'a good few miles south of the degree line where Shackleton shot his first pony' Wilson noted. The other ponies were not long for this world either; their meat was stored in depots ready for the return journey. On 4 December, Scott, following Shackleton's route, was faced with the difficult and steep Beardmore Glacier. He began the ascent to the Antarctic massif. Oates wrote in his diary: 'Saw several enormous glaciers coming down between the mountains, and some of the chasms which stopped Shackleton. And now one is here one can realise what a wonderful journey his was and the daring which prompted him.'

Amundsen passed 87 degrees South on 4 December. 'We have won. We have fought our way through storm and blizzard, and now the plateau lies before us in the sunshine ... We are tremendously pleased to see it ... the route to the Pole is free – I hope we get there soon.'

The British party, 450 kilometres behind Amundsen, were held up for days at the foot of the Beardmore Glacier by a snowstorm, and Scott complained about his bad luck: 'It is more than our share of ill-fortune ... How great may be the element of luck! No foresight – no procedure – could have prepared us for this state of affairs. Had we been ten times as experienced or certain of our aim we should not have expected such rebuffs. It's real hard luck.' They had already been travelling for 38 days, and had covered 682 kilometres; this was according to the plan, which was based on Shackleton's rate of progress, but Scott sought to beat this figure. They could not know that they were losing slightly more than six kilometres a day against Amundsen. Henry Bowers, a tough man and one of the man-hauling team waiting for better weather at the foot of the 216-kilometre glacier, wrote in his diary: 'Amundsen has probably reached the Pole by now. I hope he has not, as I regard him as a sneaking, backhanded ruffian.'

They began their ascent on 9 December. The ponies were exhausted and had to be urged on with the whip for 12 terrible hours. Ten kilometres. The column stopped and Oates shot the animals. 'Thank God the horses are now all done with, and we begin the heavier work ourselves.' At the same time Amundsen was laying down his final depot 171 kilometres before the Pole, marking it especially carefully at five-kilometre intervals. Every hundred skiing paces, the men secured black-painted planks in the ice. Every other one had a flag attached to it and was marked with a notch on its eastern side so as to show the direction to the depot. On 10 December, they set off on their 'final onslaught. 28 degrees below, southerly wind ... quite cold if the skin of our faces is chapped, but no reason to make a fuss. The terrain and our progress are first rate, as usual. Sledges and skis run smoothly over it. Helmer Hanssen, Wisting and I look frightful, because we got frostbite in our faces a few days ago in the storm. Inflammation, pain and scabs over the entire left side. Bjaaland and Hassel went behind, so they escaped this. The dogs are getting dangerous (because they are hungry) and must be regarded as enemies as soon as the sledges are left unwatched.'

On the morning of 11 December, they were still 81 kilometres away from their goal. On the same day Scott, with 648 kilometres still to go, sent his dogs back from the Beardmore Glacier. Cherry-Garrard wrote: 'They have done splendidly. It looks as if Amundsen may have hit off the right thing.'

The thought of his rival made Amundsen uneasy. It would feel like a national disgrace if they only crossed the finishing line in second place. On December 13, Hassel began to lose his nerve. 'See that black thing over there? Is that Scott?' As they went on, the object turned out to be a mirage above the ice. On 14 December, they set up camp at 89 degrees 45 minutes South. There were only 27 kilometres to go to the Pole. Bjaaland was as excited as the rest. 'Now we can look at the Pole lying down, and I can already hear the axle creak, but in the morning it will be greased. We are all excited. Will we see the English flag? God have mercy on us! I don't think we will.' That day they had to use the whip to keep the huskies off each other. 'The dogs are so hungry they are eating their own crap, and their harnesses, too, if they can get at them. They are biting the wood of the sledges.'

Roald Amundsen's assistant Helmer Hanssen stands with his dogs and sleigh at the South Pole.

On Friday 15 December, they set off with more urgency than usual. After 12.6 kilometres of fast progress, the teams reined in and the men let Amundsen go in front; at around three o'clock, he became the first man to reach the South Pole. There, 28,800 kilometres away from the Bundefjord, their journey was over. 'Well, so now we are there, and we can raise our flag at the geographical South Pole,' Amundsen wrote of the moment when he tasted victory. 'Beloved flag, we have raised you at the South Pole, and named the plain in which it lies the King Haakon VII Plateau.'

Helmer Hanssen also recorded his feelings in his diary, with a similarly reserved note. 'I was glad not to have to stare at the compass any longer in that biting wind. Throughout our southward journey we had the wind against us, but now it will come from behind.' Bjaaland's tone was different: 'We have reached the goal of our desires, and the splendid thing is we got there first; there is no English flag flying here, just the Norwegian tricolour. We have eaten and drunk our fill: seal steaks, biscuits, pemmican, and chocolate. If you knew, mother, and Susanna and T. and Sven and Helga and Hans, if you only knew that I am here at the South Pole writing to you, you would surely celebrate too.'

Later, Amundsen wrote about the conquest of the South Pole: 'I cannot say that I had reached the goal of my life. I know that would be a much more impressive thing to say, but it would not be the truth. I prefer to be honest and come right out with it – never has a man attained a goal so diametrically opposed to his wishes. The area around the North

Pole – devil take it – had fascinated me since childhood, and now here I was at the South Pole. Could anything be more crazy?'

Peary had succeeded in reaching his lifelong goal, the North Pole. Amundsen had attained the goal of another man, who was at that moment still 640 kilometres away, struggling to get off the Beardmore Glacier. Amundsen had acquired the fame of a conqueror, but this brought him no closer to his own lifelong goal. He was never to attain it – not even years later when he flew over the North Pole in an airship.

They spent three days and five hours at the Pole, continually measuring its exact geographical position so that no-one could cast doubt on their victory. Then they erected the spare tent, securing the Norwegian flag to the top of it together with the flag of the *Fram*. Amundsen placed some broken equipment and two letters inside the tent, the first to Scott, asking him to convey the second letter to the King of Norway. 'Your majesty! We have ascertained the southernmost point of the great Ross Ice Barrier as well as the point where Victoria Land and King Edward VII Land meet. We have discovered a mighty chain of mountains with peaks up to 22,000 feet high. I have taken the liberty – with your permission, I hope – of naming them the Queen Helena Range. We have found that the great inland plateau begins to slope gently downward from 89 degrees … We have named this gently sloping plateau – also I hope with Your Majesty's permission – the King Haakon VII Plateau; on which we have managed to determine the position of the Geographical South Pole.'

Then they sealed the tent and saluted the flag before turning their gaze northwards. In his diary Amundsen recorded a final greeting to the point where the lines of longitude meet, but which looks just like any other in the white surface. 'And now, dear Pole, farewell! I do not think we will ever see each other again.'

Photographed by Oates, Scott, Bowers, Wilson and Evans stand in bitter acknowledgement of their defeat. The Norwegian flag flies above the tent Amundsen had left at the Pole.

9

Triumph, Defeat and Death

'All the day dreams must go ... look after our people.'

Captain Scott

'They were not lacking in courage, determination or strength. A little more knowledge and their efforts would have succeeded.'

Roald Amundsen on Scott's Polar team

'We are now six days behind,' Scott wrote on 16 December, 'the only reason is the miserable storm.' He did not know that Amundsen had reached the Pole on the previous day, nor would he have believed it. He had found no trace of Amundsen on his route – the same route as Shackleton's – which he believed to be the only possible route up to the Polar plateau. The Norwegian must be behind him. 'We are making up the lost ground,' he wrote in his diary the following day. It was always Shackleton he measured his team's progress against. With 11 men he made his way up the enormous Beardmore Glacier, its deep rifts hidden under deep, soft snow. The men were on skis, which 'are just the right thing, but my countrymen are sluggish and full of prejudices, they were not ready for it'. He does not mention the fact that he left it up to his men to decide whether they wanted to receive instruction from Tryggve Gran in skiing techniques or not. On the 21st they were off the glacier, on the edge of the ice cap. Once more Scott sent a four-man support party back to base camp. He asked Atkinson, one of the expedition's two doctors (the other was Wilson) to come as far as he could to meet him with the dogs in March. This was the third time he had changed his instructions to the parties that were supposed to meet him on the way back from the Pole. None of these changes was clear, and they were contradictory. The men at Cape Evans, trained to obey orders to the letter without question, found them perplexing.

Scott was drawing ever closer to his lifelong goal, with two sledges and seven men, nine or sometimes ten hours a day. On 25 December Bowers wrote: 'Scott got fairly wound up and went on and on ... my breath kept fogging my glasses and our windproofs got oppressively warm and altogether things were pretty rotten. At last he stopped and said we had done 14 ¾ miles. He said, "What about fifteen miles for Christmas day?", so we gladly went on – anything definite is better than indefinite trudging.'

On the same day, a primus stove was keeping the Norwegians' tent warm. Bjaaland passed round cigars, and Wisting had made a pudding out of crumbled biscuit, powdered milk and melted snow. They had already covered 180 kilometres of the return journey. Wisting had toothache. 'So I asked

Amundsen to deal with the thing. He agreed straight away, and we got out the pliers. They were so cold they had to be wormed up on the Primus stove first. Then I kneeled in my sleeping bag and he placed himself in front of me in his own before pulling with all his might. After this horrible procedure the operation was completed successfully, and my pain was also at an end.'

Scott was as strong as a bear and drove his men on, 23 or sometimes 25 kilometres a day. Teddy Evans, Bowers, the seamen Lashly and Crean could barely manage to pull their sledge fast enough to keep up with Scott, Wilson, Edgar Evans and Oates. 'I have told them plainly that they must wrestle with the trouble and get it right for themselves.' He would have to tell his deputy that only his own sledge team would go all the way to the Pole – Wilson, Oates and Edgar Evans, the same sailor who had accompanied him to the western mountains during the *Discovery* expedition. Scott forced the pace of his own sledge.

There, 270 kilometres away from the goal, he had the sledges reconstructed, shortening them by a foot and a half to make them go better. This task that could probably have been completed in three hours at Cape Evans took all of eight hours at minus 25°, at an altitude of 3,000 metres. In the process, Evans cut his hand; until his death, the wound would not close.

'The Plateau, 3 January 1912. I have been selected to go on to the Pole with Scott.' Scott had announced his final Polar team. Oates told his mother: 'I am of course delighted but I am sorry I shall not be home for another year ... We are now within 50 miles of Shackleton's Furthest South. It is pretty cold up here and the work has been very heavy but I am very fit indeed and have lost condition less than anyone else almost. What a lot we shall have to talk about when I get back.'

The decision was made. Teddy Evans, Lashly and Crean would have to turn back. Only later would the two sailors and the man who had saved them all from shipwreck discover that for them, Scott's decision meant the difference between life and death. Once again, Scott altered the plans for the march, which would continue with five men rather than four. Bowers was a surveyor, and it would also be, said Scott, 'an immense relief to have the indefatigable little Bowers to see to all detail arrangements'. Of course, Bowers was delighted. It did not yet occur to anyone that the food supply in the depots would now have to feed five men, though the amount had been calculated for four. Later, seemingly surprised, Scott wrote: 'Cooking for five takes a seriously longer time than cooking for four. It is an item I had not considered when re-organising.' But there was not enough fuel to allow for significantly longer cooking times. As a result of a sudden whim, Scott changed his plans, and this would upset his entire strategy for the route. He did not think of the fact that Bowers had left his skis behind a couple of days' march back. There was no provision for spare skis for Scott's crew, though a spare pair was taken for each member of the Norwegian polar team. Bowers hauled the central line, and this worked well as long as the other four to his left and right were also hauling the sledge on foot. But when the snow was deep and soft and the others pulled on their skis, the team lost its rhythm. Hauling sledges, as Bowers had already discovered on the ice shelf, 'is the most back-breaking work I have ever come up against. The starting was worse than pulling as it required from ten to fifteen desperate jerks on the harness to move the sledge at all. I have never pulled so hard, or so nearly crushed my inside into my backbone by the everlasting jerking with all my strength on the canvas band round my unfortunate tummy'. Scott appreciated the endurance of Bowers, a strong little man, as a sledge-hauler.

On 4 January those who were going home gave three cheers and watched Scott and his four companions until they had disappeared over the horizon. They turned round and headed back to Cape Evans, laden with letters. One was for Kathleen Scott, who was in the midst of a brief but intense affair with Fridtjof Nansen in a Berlin hotel. Scott wrote to his wife: 'I have led this business – not nominally but actually – so that no man will or can say I wasn't fit to lead through the last lap.'

Hour after hour they pulled their sledge through the pathless white waste, day after day. 'The marching is growing dreadfully monotonous.' Mile after mile, the horizon always remained just as far off. In silence, the men held the hauling straps taut, 18 kilometres a day. Then they crossed an area full of sastrugi, ridges of frozen snow polished by the wind as hard as glass that defeated Scott's skiing technique.

He decided to continue without skis the following day – without consulting the others. On 7 January they left their skis behind at their camp, and they could all pull evenly. But then the men began to argue about the value of the skis. Scott ended the dispute by returning to the camp to fetch them. That day, they only made 16 kilometres.

On 7 January, shortly before midnight, the Norwegians reached their first depot on the ice shelf at 85 degrees 5 minutes South. This meant that Amundsen had enough supplies on his sledges for 35 days – more than enough food for men and animals to get back safely to Framheim. And after each further degree of latitude, he would come to a depot carefully marked on all four points of the compass with flags and boards. They could not miss them, and the way back to the Bay of Whales lay ahead, a pleasant journey. Amundsen had won the contest once and for all.

On 9 January, Captain Scott felt he was the victor; he wrote in his diary in block capitals 'RECORD!' Scott had left behind what was for him the magical point of 88 degrees 23 minutes South, 162 degrees East, the point where Shackleton had had to turn back exactly three years previously. 'We have shot our bolt … Whatever regrets may be, we have done our best,' Shackleton had written at the time. Finally Scott had beaten his rival, and decided the British contest on the Antarctic continent. But that did nothing to make the last stretch to the Pole any easier for him. He had won one race, but now the other one, forced on him by Amundsen, occupied his thoughts more and more. Perhaps there really was another route up from the ice shelf to the high plateau? What if Amundsen was waiting for him at the Pole?

They had insufficient fuel on their sledge, so they had to be economical with what there was, and largely do without melting snow for drinking water. Anyone who was thirsty put a handful of snow in his mouth, but this was not enough to provide the amount of water the body needed. The effects made themselves felt – physical and mental weakness. Edgar Evans had not spoken for days, cowed, pulling weakly in his harness. His hand oozed pus. All the men complained of the cold, and of their perceptibly decreasing physical strength. Scott's biographers would later explain this as the result of an unbalanced diet, which was particularly lacking in B vitamins. Oates also found it difficult to shake off depressive moments. On 15 January, when they were within 54 kilometres of the Pole, he wrote: 'My pemmican must have disagreed with me at breakfast, for coming along I felt very depressed and homesick.'

Four days before this, a pair of skuas had flown over the sledges of the Norwegians, the first sign of life they had seen, and they were greeted with a loud cheer. Bjaaland fired a volley from his revolver before describing his joy in his diary: 'Hello, greetings, dear skua-crow. How are you? Fly back to Lindstrøm and tell him that we will be there in 20 days and eat up all his pancakes and the beef and the fruit, even if it is just green plums.'

It was more than vitamin deficiency that made the British expedition feel uncertain as they got nearer and nearer to knowing for sure whether they would be first or only second to reach the Pole. Oates expressed the thought that was oppressing them all: 'The only appalling possibility, the sight of the Norwegian flag forestalling ours.' Bowers was the first to spot it, a dark blurred speck on the horizon. Half an hour later, they were standing before a black flag that Amundsen had planted five kilometres away from the Pole as a signal for the British party. It was 16 January, about five o'clock. The men could see ski tracks and the prints of a large number of dogs. The Empire had arrived too late. Scott withdrew to camp together with his men. 'We're not a very happy party tonight,' reported Oates: 'Amundsen – I must say that man must have his head screwed on right. The Norskies seem to have had a comfortable trip with their dog teams, very different to our wretched man-hauling'. Bowers wrote: 'It is sad that we have been forestalled by the Norwegians, but I am glad that we have done it by good British man-haulage. That is the traditional British sledging method and this is the greatest journey done by man. If ever a journey has been accomplished by honest sweat ours has.'

Evans was struggling with his injured hand and Wilson tried to ease the crew's feeling of defeat, 'Amundsen has beaten us in so far as he made a race of it. We have done what we came for all the same and as our programme was made out.' Wilson spoke the truth, but still he could not comfort Scott. 'It is a terrible disappointment. Many bitter thoughts come. Tomorrow we must march on to the Pole and then hasten home with all the speed we can compass. All the day dreams must go; it will be a wearisome return.'

On 17 January 1912 at about half past six in the evening, the men stood at the Pole, 34 days after the Norwegians. The sky was overcast and the wind mercilessly fierce. Scott seemed apathetic, as he does in the photos they took of their arrival. 'The Pole. Yes, but under very different circumstances from those expected. We have had a horrible day – add to our disappointment a head wind 4 to 5, with a temperature -22 degrees, and companions labouring on with cold feet and hands. Great God! This is an awful place and terrible enough for us to have laboured to it without the reward of priority … the cold chills one to the bone … There is very little that is different from the monotony of past days … Well, it is something to have got here, and the wind may be our friend tomorrow … Now for the run home.'

They discovered the Norwegians' spare tent and Scott opened the letter addressed to him. 'Dear Captain Scott, As you probably are the first to reach this area after us, I will ask you kindly to forward this letter to King Haakon VII. If you can use any of the articles left in the tent please do not hesitate to do so. With kind regards I wish you a safe return. Yours truly, Roald Amundsen.' The tone of the letter cut Scott to the quick, perhaps even undermining his will to survive. He had arrived second on his Polar journey; was it as a postman that he was now to come first?

Bowers was delighted with some reindeer-skin gloves that the Norwegians had left behind in their tent, having lost his own dogskin ones. Scott put a message in the tent to record their arrival at the southern meeting point of the lines of longitude before sealing it. 'We built a cairn, put up our poor slighted Union Jack, and photographed ourselves – mighty cold work, all of it. We have turned our back now on the goal of our ambition with sore feelings and must face our 800 miles of solid dragging – and good-bye to most of the day dreams! 19 January 1912. Scott.'

Listlessly they left the place of their defeat; in the first three weeks they marched 16 kilometres daily, retracing their tracks. The wind was behind them, and they put up a little sail on the sledge, going slightly downhill across the plateau, doing their best not to lose sight of the tracks they had made on the way there. The sun, however, shone against them from the north, turning the ice and snow into one indistinguishable glare. Then they had to remove their harnesses and scratch about in the snow to look for the marks. Amundsen led his men back at night, with the sun behind them, to the south. Scott continued running against the sun. If it was obscured by clouds, this did not make it any easier to find their own traces, as they had already in many cases been blown away. Storm clouds were now appearing more and more often over the polar cap, leading the temperatures to sink below minus 30°. 'We had the dickens of a time getting up the tent, cold fingers all round.'

While the five men were struggling to make their way across the high Antarctic plateau back to Cape Evans, the other five – Amundsen's party – had already reached their

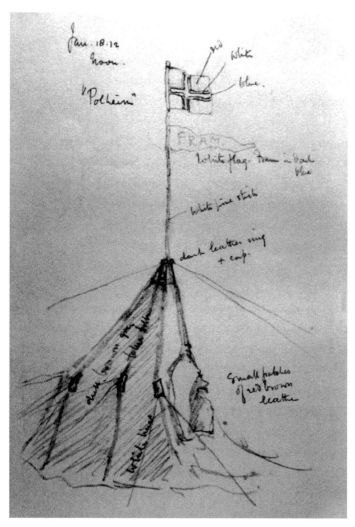

A sketch of the Norwegian expedition's tent drawn by Captain Scott. A personal memento of the crushing discovery that his party had been beaten to the South Pole by Amundsen's team more than a month earlier.

base camp at the edge of the ice shelf. 'Framheim appeared just as we had left it, in the morning sun' – Amundsen's sober diary entry for the 26 January 1912, 4 a.m. On the following day the *Fram* anchored in the Bay of Whales, having arrived punctually on the 9th before being driven back out into the Ross Sea by storms and ice. Now they loaded her with the most valuable equipment and 37 dogs. On the evening of 30 January, Amundsen left the hut and his ship made its way out of the Bay of Whales. 'A heavy moment to leave Framheim. A more splendid and cosy winter quarters no one has had. It was the best and cheeriest winter quarters there has ever been. It looked brand new when we left, as Lindstrøm had given it a thorough clean.'

'I shall be jolly glad to pick up my dear old ski.' On 31 January, after Bowers had marched around 650 kilometres through snow and over ice, he was finally able to strap his skis back on beneath his boots. Four days later they reached the edge of the polar plateau and began to descend the Beardmore Glacier; it was just a few kilometres down to the first depot at the top of the glacier. There was now not much leeway, just five days' food for five days' travel, exactly the same period it had taken them to get from the middle depot on the outward journey. Perhaps, Scott thought, the same distance could be traversed more quickly downhill. In any case, he had not thought of a safety margin. The next morning they continued to go down, with sunny weather after weeks of cold wind. On 9 February, the same day the *Fram* crossed the Antarctic Circle, Scott interrupted their descent to collect geological samples, loading the sledge with around 30 kilos of mineral-rich rock that he intended to take back to Cape Evans. His curiosity got the better of his good sense, meaning that he and his men lost valuable time that they no longer had. On the following day Scott realised that their food was running out, and they needed to reach the middle Beardmore depot by the 12th at the latest. 'We are in a rather nasty hole tonight. Got among bad crevasses and pressure, all blue ice. We struggled in this chaos until about 9 p.m., when we were absolutely done,' Oates wrote on 12 February. They had lost their way, and ended up in one of the most dangerous parts of the glacier, as if they were walking into a trap. Evans broke through encrusted snow bridges twice, injuring his head and suffering concussion. Luckily, the others were able to pull him out of the crevasses. Oates wrote: 'It's an extraordinary thing about Evans, he's lost his guts and behaves like an old woman or worse. He's quite worn out with the work, and how he's going to do the 400 odd miles we've still got to do, I don't know. We have got to find the depot.' Scott knew it all too well. Evans was the only one who managed to get any sleep at all during that night between all the crevasses; the others waited impatiently for morning. When it arrived, it was shrouded in fog, making the men shiver and blocking their descent. But they had to keep going; there was no alternative. Wilson caught sight of the depot flag in a break in the fog, and they were saved once again. It was, Scott wrote, 'the worst experience of the trip and gave a horrid feeling of insecurity. In future food must be worked so that we do not run so short if the weather fails us. We mustn't get into a hole like this again.'

Evans was suffering from frostbite and showing the early signs of scurvy. 'Evans has dislodged two finger nails … his hands are really bad, and to my surprise he shows signs of losing heart over it – which makes me much disappointed in him.' He seemed apathetic, and babbled incomprehensible fragments of sentences like a small child.

On the 13th they set off for the lower glacier depot. They only had enough food left for three days. 'We don't know our distance from the next depot, we are pulling for food. We have reduced food, also sleep; feeling rather done.' Evans still stumbled about in the traces with the others, until he collapsed on the 16th. Oates described what happened: 'Evans first had to get out of his harness and hold on to the sledge and later said he could not get on. If he does not get by tomorrow God knows how we're going to get him home. We cannot possibly take him on the sledge.'

The following morning Evans could no longer manage his boots. Scott and the others did not know how to help their companion; they had to get on, reach the next depot as quickly as possible, and they could not put Evans on the sledge as well as the rocks it was carrying. They left him behind having told him to follow on as soon as he could. After lunch there was no sign of him, and Scott and Oates went back up. They found Evans crawling on all fours in the snow. Wilson and Bowers brought the empty sledge; Evans was taken down to the tent. It was 17 February 1912. On the following day Scott wrote a declaration in his diary: 'I take this opportunity of saying that we have stuck to our sick companions. In case of Edgar Evans the safety of the remainder seemed to demand his abandonment, but Providence mercifully removed him at the critical moment. Evans was unconscious when he was carried into the tent, and he died in the night, without having regained consciousness.'

They broke camp at once, and made their way over several ice ridges to find the lower depot, where they had their first proper meal after seven days of short rations. Then, according to Scott, 'we gave ourselves 5 hours' sleep after the horrible night' before they finally left the Beardmore Glacier behind them. Then they came to the Shambles Camp on the southern edge of the Ross Shelf Ice, where Oates had shot the ponies on the way up. They scraped a carcass out of the encrusted snow and ate their fill for the first time in ages. The effects did not last long, as their bodies were emaciated from constant effort. Cape Evans was a long way off, more than 600 kilometres, and the Antarctic winter was drawing closer. They had to fight for every kilometre, every man for himself. 'Heavy toiling all day, inspiring gloomiest thoughts at all times. We never won a march of 8 ½ miles with greater difficulty, but we can't go on like this. Fuel is woefully short. Pray God we have no further set-backs. It is a critical position. We may find ourselves in safety at next depot, but there is a horrid element of doubt.' Scott knew that they were fighting for their lives. It was no longer a question of bringing the expedition to a dignified end in spite of their defeat. The temperature fell further, to an average of minus 35°, and the next problem had been gradually becoming apparent over the past ten or eleven days – Oates. It was taking him more than an hour in the mornings to put on his boots, which were always frozen solid. His wound suffered ten years previously when a bullet had smashed his thigh during the Boer War had reopened, and his leg was devastated by the frost and the first signs of scurvy. The others also had trouble getting their swollen feet into their boots, and out of consideration for his companions Oates had said nothing about his pains. He had gritted his teeth, and just become slightly quieter. Now he could conceal it no longer. He had lost all his strength and could no longer pull in harness with the others; he staggered about next to the sledge on his moribund feet. 'Poor Soldier nearly done,' Scott wrote. 'It is pathetic enough because we can do nothing for him. We none of us expected these terribly low temperatures.'

The feet. For Edgar Evans, too, his feet were the origin of death spreading through his body; Oates knew it and suspected what Scott was writing in his diary, that he had 'become a terrible hindrance and he can never get through. He asked Wilson if he had a chance this morning, and of course Bill had to say he didn't know. In point of fact he has none. Apart from him, if he went under now, I doubt whether we could get through. The weather conditions are awful, and our gear gets steadily more icy and difficult to manage. At the same time of course poor Titus is the greatest handicap. Poor chap! poor chap. It is too pathetic to watch him.'

On the same day, 4 March, the crew of the *Fram* sighted land, reaching Hobart, in Tasmania, three days later. Amundsen went ashore, having forbidden the others to leave the ship until he had cabled his message confirming the conquest of the South Pole, and took a room in Hadley's Orient Hotel. 'With my peaked cap and my blue jumper they took me for a landlubber and I got a grotty little room.' As agreed, he cabled his brother Leon: 'Pole reached 14 – 17 December. All well'. This was printed on front pages the world over, and the *New York Times* celebrated the achievement with a huge headline. 'The whole world has now been discovered.' But Amundsen had another battle to conclude before he basked in the world's acclamation, his quarrel with Johansen. He dismissed Johansen from the crew on the grounds of mutiny, compelling him to return to Norway alone while the *Fram* sailed on to Buenos Aires. Before Johansen's arrival in Christiania Fridtjof Nansen and the Royal Norwegian Geographical Association had received urgent letters from Amundsen dismissing him as a quarrelsome ne'er-do-well. It was as a defeated man that he returned to a country that only welcomed victors. His drinking did nothing to help his reputation, though it may have helped ease the pain. On 4 January 1913, Johansen put his army revolver in his mouth and pulled the trigger. 'Perhaps it was the best thing that could happen to him, the poor devil,' opined Thorvald Nilsen.

Scott's diary entry for 9 March 1912: 'Shortage on our allowance all round. I don't know that anyone is to blame

– but generosity and thoughtfulness has not been abundant. The dogs which would have been our salvation have obviously failed. It's a miserable jumble.' Scott was a victim of the British naval tradition that beat unconditional obedience to orders into all in its ranks, while driving out all initiative. His instructions, altered several times during the outward march, for dog-drawn sledges to meet the returning Polar party at this or that location, were taken by the crew at base camp for what they were: contradictory statements by the commander that no-one was quite sure what to do about. They were certainly not orders that could be carried out to the letter. In addition, the officers and scientific personnel at Cape Evans were busy with their own tasks, but the other ranks had no similar instructions. It was the scientist Cherry-Garrard who then set off after all with the Russian dog-driver Girev on 25 February to One Ton Camp in the belief that his journey was a sort of welcoming mission for the victorious polar party. From 4 March onwards, the two men waited for Scott at One Ton Camp for six days. On 10 March they returned with their dogs to Cape Evans, while Oates was struggling in his agony 120 kilometres to the south. At some point he gave up, and handed his diary over to Wilson, requesting that he should ensure it was given to his mother. And he asked Wilson for the morphine from his medical bag. 'Our record is clear, 'Wilson wrote.

March 17th was Oates's 32nd birthday, and he was preparing for his death. On the night of 18 March 1912, as Scott, Bowers and Wilson lay sleepless in their damp sleeping bags, Oates crawled over his companions' legs and out of the tent. No-one stopped him. 'He died like a man and a soldier, without a word of complaint.' Those were Wilson's words to Mrs Oates. Scott wrote that 'his regiment would be pleased with the bold way he met his death. We knew that poor Oates was walking to his death, but we knew it was the act of a brave man and an English gentleman'.

Scott, Wilson and Bowers dragged themselves northwards for another three days, passing 80 degrees South, and on 21 March they set up camp barely 20 kilometres away from One Ton Camp. They did not mention the fact that they would already have reached safety if Scott had set up the camp at 80 degrees, and not 79 degrees 28 minutes, in order to save the life of a pony. They were too busy trying to survive, as their reserves of food and fuel dwindled down to almost nothing. Scott feared gangrene in his frozen toes. 'Amputation is the least I can hope for now, but will the trouble spread?' He ordered Wilson 'to hand out the means to end our torments, so that everyone would know what to do if it came to it. We have 30 opium tablets apiece and he is left with a tube of morphine. So far the tragical side of our story.'

They lay in their sleeping bags for nine days when they should have been going on, while strong gusts of wind from the Polar plateau drove snowstorms down over the shelf ice. Their fuel was gone, with just a little food left, enough for another day or two if they cut their rations down to the bone. Frostbite drove all feeling from their legs and tore strips of skin off their faces. '22 and 23 March: Blizzard bad as ever

– Wilson and Bowers unable to start – to-morrow last chance – must be near the end. Have decided it shall be natural – we shall march for the depot and die in our tracks.'

They remained in the tent and continued to write farewell letters, as they had been doing for several days.

'I fear we must go,' Scott wrote to Sir Edward Speyer, a London banker and treasurer of the expedition. 'I was not too old for this job. It was the younger men that went under first …' 'We are setting a good example to our countrymen, if not by getting in a tight place, by facing it like men when we get there,' he wrote to Admiral Sir Francis Bridgeman. The words are different, but the message is always the same: 'We are showing that Englishmen can still die with a bold spirit, fighting it out to the end. I think this makes an example for Englishmen of the future.' Or: 'We shall die like gentlemen. I think this will show the Spirit of pluck and power to endure has not passed out of our race.'

With the British public in mind, he wrote: 'The causes of the disaster are not due to faulty organisation but due to misfortune in all risks which had to be undertaken – the loss of the pony transport, the weather, the soft snow in lower reaches of glacier … I do not think human beings ever came through such a month as we have come through. We should have got through but for the sickening of Captain Oates, and a shortage of fuel in our depots for which I cannot account.'

In 1913, when news of Scott's death reached the British public and his diaries and letters were published, his end was taken as an example of British greatness and virtue, and the

British defeat on the Antarctic continent was transformed into a heroic national legend, at a time when the country was on the brink of war. The British Empire would soon have need of men who were not afraid to die for the greater glory of their country.

Unlike Scott, Bowers had neither the strength nor the talent to turn himself into a future legend. His farewell has a quiet tone: 'My trust is still in Him and in the abounding Grace of my Lord and Saviour whom you brought me to trust in. I should so like to come through for your dear sake. It is splendid to pass however with such companions as I have. There will be no shame however and you will know that I have struggled to the end. Oh, how I do feel for you when you hear all, you will know that for me the end was peaceful as it is only sleep in the cold.'

The storm blew snowdrifts up around the tent and dispersed them again. Wilson, Bowers and Scott were freezing, and hunger was making them more and more sluggish. Scott's final entry was dated 29 March 1912. 'Since the 21st we have had a continuous gale from W.S.W. and S.W. Every day we have been ready to start for our depot 11 miles away, but outside the door of the tent it remains a scene of whirling drift. I do not think we can hope for any better things now. We shall stick it out to the end, but we are getting weaker, of course, and the end cannot be far. It seems a pity, but I do not think I can write more.' There was no more strength in his hands, and his fingers were raw from frostbite. 'For God's sake look after our people. R. Scott'

Eight months later, on 11 November 1912, the green tent was found. Scott had thrown back the flaps of his sleeping bag and put his arm around Wilson. The faces of the dead men appeared as though peacefully asleep. The tent was collapsed over the bodies, burying them as they had been found, in their sleeping bags. At the same time, Amundsen had just finished his account of the discovery of the South Pole, having abandoned the plan of drifting to the North Pole in the *Fram*. The book came out in 1912, and began with the following words: 'Here I sit shaded by palms, surrounded by luxuriant vegetation, enjoying the most delectable fruits – and writing the story of Antarctic exploration.'

we shall stick it out
to the end but we
are getting weaker of
course and the end
cannot be far.

It seems a pity but
I do not think I can
write more —

R. Scott

Last Entry —

For Gods sake look
after our people

The last entry in Captain Scott's journal.

Bibliography

Amundsen, Roald, *Die Eroberung des Südpols. Die norwegische Südpolfahrt mit dem Fram 1910–1912* 1-11 (München: 1912).

——, *Die Jagd nach dem Nordpol. Mit dem Flugzeug zum 88* (Berlin: 1925).

——, *Die Nordwest-Passage. Meine Polarfahrt auf der Gjöa 1903 bis 1907*. (München: 1908).

——, *Mein Leben als Entdecker* (Leipzig-Wien: 1929).

Arnesen, Odd, *Roald Amundsen, wie er war. Eine Schilderung seines Lebens* (Stuttgart: 1931).

Cook, Frederick A, *Die erste Südpolarnacht 1898–1899. Bericht über die Entdeckungsreise der «Belgica» in der Südpolarregion (1900)* (Kempten: 1903).

Gwynn, Stephen, *Captain Scott* (Lane, London: 1929).

Huntford, Roland, *Scott und Amundsen; Dramatischer Kampf um d. Südpol (Athenäum, Königstein/*Ts.: 1980).

——, *The Last Place on Earth* (Modern Library, New York: 1999).

—— (ed), *Die Amundsen-Photographien. Expeditionen ins ewige Eis* (Braunschweig: 1989).

Marc, Pierre, and Vladimír Novák, *Amundsen und Scott am Südpol* (Bohem-Press, Zürich: 1992).

Scott, Robert Falcon, *Letzte Fahrt; Scott, (R{obert Falcon},)*
Kapitän ; Scotts Tageb. 2. Aufl. Mit 37 Textzeichngn v. Willi
Daum (Brockhaus, Leipzig: 1951).

———, *Scott's Last Expedition* : in 2 vols /arranged by
Leonard Huxley. With a pref. by Sir Clements R[obert]
Markham. With photograv. frontispieces, 6 orig.
sketches by Dr. E. A. Wilson, 18 pl., 260 ill., from
photogr. taken by Herbert G. Ponting … ; panoramas
and maps (Smith, Elder & Co., London : 1913).

———, *Scott's Last Expedition*; *The personal journal of Captain*
R(obert) F(alcon) Scott on his journey to the South Pole. With
biograph. introd. by Sir J[ames] M[atthew] Barrie and
a pref. by Sir Clements R[obert] Markham (Murray,
London: 1923).

———, *Scott's Last Expedition ; The journals of Captain R(obert)*
F(alcon) Scott. Arranged by Leonard Huxley (Beacon
Press, Boston: 1957).

———, *The Voyage of the 'Discovery'.*With 260 ill., photograv.
frontisp., 12 pl., panoramas and maps. In 2 vols (Smith,
Elder, & Co., London: 1905).

Wilson, Edward, *Diary of the Terra Nova Expedition to the*
Antarctic, 1910–1912 ; An account of Scott's last expedition
ed. from the original mss. in the Scott Polar Research
Inst. and the British Museum by H[arold] G[odfrey]
R[udolf] King (Blandford Press, London: 1972).

Yelverton, David E, *Antarctica Unveiled : Scott's first*
expedition and the quest for the unknown continent
(University of Colorado Press, Boulder: 2000).

Index

04051
18.00 5.99
Postscript